Berlitz®

Berlin

KU-215-552

- A ☛ in the text denotes a highly recommended sight
- A complete A–Z of practical information starts on p.104
- Extensive mapping throughout: on cover flaps and in text

Berlitz Publishing Company, Inc.

Princeton   Mexico City   Dublin   Eschborn   Singapore

Text:	Brigitte Lee, Jack Messenger and Jack Altman
Editor:	Sarah Hudson, Claire Evans Calder
Photography:	Jon Davison
Layout:	Media Content Marketing, Inc.
Cartography:	Visual Image

Thanks to Verkehrsamt Berlin for their invaluable help and advice in the preparation of this guide.

Found an error we should know about? Our editor would be happy to hear from you, and a postcard would do. Although we make every effort to ensure the accuracy of all the information in this book, changes do occur.

ISBN 2-8315-6413-1
Revised 1998 – First Printing January 1998

Printed in Switzerland by Weber SA, Bienne
019/801 REV

CONTENTS

BERLIN

BERLIN AND THE BERLINERS

Is there a city more evocative of modern European history than Berlin? Since it first became Germany's capital, it has excited pride for its strength, admiration for its culture, hatred as the center of Hitler's tyranny, compassion as a bastion of post-war freedom, and fear as a focus of Cold War conflict. More than any other European capital, Berlin symbolizes the immense changes wrought in Western and Eastern Europe as the 20th century draws to a close.

For each emotion which the name Berlin evokes, the city has appropriate symbols. The noble Charlottenburg Palace and the monuments on Unter den Linden honour the formidable Prussian past, while the Brandenburg Gate proclaims the city's regained unity. The Reichstag recalls united Germany's attempts at a parliamentary democracy, while the gigantic Olympic Stadium expresses only too well the bombast of Hitler's dictatorship. The chaos and destruction he wreaked find their deliberate reminder in the bombed-out shell of the Kaiser Wilhelm Memorial Church, while the determination of the Jewish community to forge a stronger identity is symbolized in the restored magnificence of the New Synagogue.

Relics of the Old Divide

The eastern districts of the city — Mitte, Pankow, Friedrichshain, and Prenzlauer Berg — form essentially the old densely populated center whose tenements (disparagingly referred to as *Mietskasernen*, literally meaning "rental barracks") inspired the 1920s proletarian theater of Erwin Piscator and Bertolt Brecht. When Berlin was divided up at the end of the Second World War, it was appropriate that the

Soviet sector devoted to the Communist experiment should take in a large number of the working-class areas, while West Berlin had at its center the eminently bourgeois neighbourhood of Charlottenburg.

Today, now that the post-reunification euphoria has worn off, the city still shows visible scars from that old division. Two sets of people psychologically attuned to different economic and social systems were suddenly thrust together, and hitherto unforeseen problems emerged. As tens of thousands of East Germans came to settle in the West, entitling them to "adjustment" money, housing subsidies, and job retraining from the Bonn government, the financial burden of reunification now began to trouble West Germans, while a small minority of disgruntled West Berliners even began to wish that the Wall had never been knocked down.

For the inhabitants of East Berlin, too, the merger with the West was less than idyllic. The sudden impact of the West's free-market economic system has been in some cases disastrous, with people losing such previously enjoyed benefits as controlled rents and job security. It is taking a long time, plus an enormous ongoing investment for, in Willy Brandt's now immortal words, "what belongs together to grow together."

Reconstruction and Renewal

The collapse of the Wall and the integration of two independent cities has led to a wealth and diversity of culture. With no less than three opera houses, three major symphony orchestras, and two national art galleries, Berlin is justifiably proud of its renewed artistic vigour. The Kulturforum in the Tiergarten is in the process of expanding its concert halls and galleries, the magnificent Museuminsel in the middle of the River Spree has been resored, and a dynamic new extension has been added to the Berlin Museum, reopening in

1998. Western Berlin's Schaubühne, along with the Berliner Ensemble and Deutsches Theater from the East, now make up one of the world's most formidable theater establishments promoting both classical tradition and the avant-garde.

With the Berlin Film Festival as its flagship, cinema is now resuming the excitement of its great creative period in the 1920s, while Berlin's own "Hollywood," the Babelsberg Studios (near Potsdam), has become the main focus of renewed activity.

Well over 100,000 students, professors and other academic personnel are at work in the city's three universities and numerous research institutes. Adding to the considerable investment in textiles, engineering, chemicals and electrical equipment, many large companies from Germany, Japan and America have set up new operations in the hope of cashing in on Berlin's future.

Signs of transformation can be seen everywhere you go. Some cynical Berliners claim that their city is being transformed into Europe's largest building site, but what the construction will yield is office, retail, and living space to accommo-

Reunification has inspired many Berliners to contemplate the past as well as the future.

date a growing population eventually boosted by the completion of the move from Bonn of government ministers and civil servants in the year 2000. There are ambitious projects for the Reichstag, once more the seat of unified Germany's parliament (one of the projects, Hungarian artist Christo's feat of wrapping the building in silver fabric, took place in June 1995). Potsdamer Platz, a hive of activity in the days of the Weimar Republic, is now the focus of energetic debate over proposed office development, while a huge American Business Center, complete with shops, offices, and apartments is rising from the former Checkpoint Charlie. Gleaming new shopping malls have recently been constructed around Friedrichstraße, and old, delapidated buildings in the east of the city have been transformed into art galleries, exclusive fashion boutiques and trendy cafés.

Breathing Space

Despite its stone, steel, and glass, Berlin is the greenest metropolis in Europe, with almost 40 percent of its area covered by lakes and rivers, parkland and woods. Besides the Tiergarten and the River Spree in the city center, the southwest suburbs have the forest of the Grunewald, the River Havel, and the Wannsee, while the north has the Tegel forest and lake. Small garden colonies abound, with flourishing farming communities, such as Lübars, set inside the city boundaries. To all of this, eastern Berlin adds its own Großer Müggelsee as well as the woods and parkland around Treptow and Köpenick.

The Hinterland itself is also accessible for delightful excursions. Potsdam, at the other end of the Glienicke Bridge, lies within easy reach for a visit to Frederick the Great's Sanssouci Palace, with its extensive grounds; or you could go walking in the surrounding forests and parks of Charlottenhof, Petzow, and Werder, try a spot of boating on the

Templiner Lake, or even make a pilgrimage to the monastery of Lehnin near Brandenburg.

Young at Heart

Beyond sightseeing, the most fascinating thing about Berlin is its people. Throughout the city's turbulent history, the individualism, courage, and wit of Berliners has elicited the admiration of the watching world. A preconceived notion of Germans as a whole, but Prussians in particular, has often presented them as a cool and unfeeling people. However, such notions are quickly dispelled by the warmth

Unter den Linden is fast becoming a showcase for German technology and design.

and good humour that is exhibited by many of the city's people.

Younger Berlin's so-called "alternative scene" has revived the city's 1920s reputation of lively and wildly independent-minded creativity, sometimes foundering in disillusioned nihilism in its strongholds, the working-class districts of Neukölln and Kreuzberg. Also to be found in these two districts is Berlin's large community of *Gastarbeiter* (so-called "guest workers"), most of them from Turkey, and adding considerable colour and flavour to the city's social and gastronomic life. Although the city has not escaped the wave of xenophobia and extreme right-wing violence that has swept across the country as a whole, it generally enjoys greater tolerance of ethnic diversity than any other city in Germany.

The city's renewed status as capital of a united Germany has strengthened its ties with the international community, while memories of its past still remain in the omnipresent memorials to victims both of the Third Reich and the Cold War. What exactly will happen in Berlin in the future is difficult to predict, but it is certain that some agonizing decisions will need to be taken as the city attempts to cope with the enormous political change that has transformed it. Visitors to Berlin over the coming years will feel a mixture of privilege and awe at witnessing an exciting new city in the making.

Berlin's cultural diversity is celabrated in the rich artistic life of the German capital.

A BRIEF HISTORY

The German capital became a municipality during the 1200s, ironically as a divided city. In those days the two rival halves were in no rush to unite. The fishermen of Cölln, whose name survives in the modern borough of Neukölln, lived on an island in the River Spree. The townships that comprise the modern Mitte district grew up around market places over which the people's churches, the Nikolaikirche and Marienkirche, still tower today. With the fortress of Burg Köpenick providing a common defense to the south, Cölln and Berlin formed a trade center between Magdeburg and Poznan.

In a region inhabited by the Slavonic Sorbs, the population of the city was overwhelmingly German by the 13th century, comprising enterprising merchants hailing from the northern Rhineland, Westphalia, and Lower Saxony, with latecomers from Thuringia and the Harz. Berlin and Cölln came together in 1307 in order to lead the Brandenburg region's defences and defeat the robber barons who were terrorizing merchants and local peasants. The prosperous city joined the Hanseatic League, trading in rye, wool, and oak timber and providing an entrepôt for skins and furs from eastern Europe. Apparently living was easy in the 15th century, as historian Trithemius noted: "Life here consists of nothing but eating and drinking."

Berlin continued as a virtually autonomous outpost of the German empire until 1448, when Brandenburg's Kurfürst (Prince Elector) Friedrich II took over control of the city after crushing the citizens' violent resistance, the so-called *Berliner Unwillen*. He was a member of the Hohenzollern dynasty that was to hold sway here for over 450 years.

The independent spirit of the Berliners made itself felt during the Reformation in the 16th century. The people were tired of paying the tribute exacted by the Catholic church. At a time when citizens of the other German principalities had to observe the religion of their prince, in 1539 Berliners were successful in pressuring Prince Elector Joachim II to accept the Protestant creed as preached by Martin Luther.

Like the rest of Germany, the city was devastated by the Thirty Years' War (1618–1648). Its Brandenburg rulers tried to befriend both the Protestant and Catholic armies but instead made enemies of both, leaving unfortified Berlin to pay the price.

Frederick the Great presides majestically over the eastern end of Unter den Linden.

Prussia — and Napoleon

With his ambition of uniting the states of Brandenburg and Prussia, it was the Great Elector Friedrich Wilhelm (1640–1688) who prepared Berlin to become a strong capital, and fortified it as a garrison town. The first newcomers were 50 wealthy Jewish families who had been expelled from Vienna in 1671. Then 14 years later 5,600 Huguenot Protestants arrived after being driven out of France by the revocation of the Edict of Nantes. At a time when France was considered the cultural master of

Europe, these sophisticated merchants and highly skilled craftsmen — among them jewellers, tailors, chefs, and restaurant-owners — brought a new refinement to the town.

This was further enhanced by the Great Elector's son who in 1701 crowned himself in Königsberg (now Kaliningrad) King Friedrich *in* (not *of*) Prussia. Prompted by Sophie Charlotte, his wife, the king founded academies for the arts and sciences in Berlin. Baroque master Andreas Schlüter (see page 52) was commissioned to redesign the royal palace, which was knocked down in 1951 to make way for East Germany's Palast der Republik. Sophie Charlotte's residence, the grand Schloß Charlottenburg, has survived as a model of the era's elegance.

Friedrich Wilhelm I (1713–1740) despised the baroque glitter of his parents' court, and subjected the previously easy-going Berliners to a frugal, rigid concept of *Preussentum* (Prussianness), that is, unquestioning obedience to the ruler and his administrators, and sharply defined class distinctions, affirming the supremacy of the aristocracy and officer class and that of soldiers over civilians in general.

A King and Cabbages

An English cousin referred to Friedrich Wilhelm I as "my brother the Sergeant," and the nickname stuck. The Soldier King spent his life in uniform and his courtiers followed suit. He had two obsessions: corporal punishment for the troops and washing his hands wherever he went.

Irascible and deeply religious, he was simple in his personal tastes, finding greatest pleasure in strictly male company over a pipe and a tankard of beer — wine struck him as too expensive. When he came to the throne, a wag's graffiti on the palace wall pinpointed the costs of his parents' extravagance: "This castle is for rent and the royal residence of Berlin for sale." To pay off the debts, he cut court officials' salaries from 250,000 silver thalers to 50,000, sold the opulent coronation robes, melted down the palace silver, and tore the flowers out of the Schloß Charlottenburg Park and replaced them with a far more practical crop: cabbages.

Friedrich der Große (Frederick the Great, 1740–1786), king *of* (not just *in*) Prussia, took his realm to the forefront of European politics and had little time for Berlin. He concentrated on turning his beloved Potsdam into a mini-Versailles, where French was spoken and Voltaire became his official philosopher-in-residence. He rarely appeared in Berlin except to garner public support — and taxes — after his return from costly wars with the Silesians, Russians, and Austrians. He did, nevertheless, leave the German capital an enduring legacy with the monumental Forum Fridericianum laid out on Unter den Linden by his architect von Knobelsdorff.

The armies of Frederick's successors proved to be no match for Napoleon's Grande Armée, however, and as the French advanced through eastern Germany in 1806, Berlin's bureaucracy, court, and bourgeoisie fled to the country. No troops were left to defend the city from its invaders, and Napoleon's march through the Brandenburg Gate into Berlin kindled a new flame of German patriotism.

There's no doubt Prussian military prowess helped shape Berlin's past and determine its future.

Capital of Germany

Defying the two-year French occupation, philosopher Johann Gottlieb Fichte exhorted the German people to assume their rightful destiny as a nation. Drummers were ordered to drown out his fiery speeches at the Royal Academy.

One of the uniting forces for the nationalist movement after the defeat of Napoleon were the *Lesecafés* (reading cafés) such as Spargnapani and Kranzler. They were a rendezvous for the intelligentsia who met to read foreign and provincial newspapers and glean information withheld in the heavily censored Berlin press.

Meanwhile, the accelerating industrial revolution had produced a new Berlin proletariat of 50,000 workers. In the wake of the 1848 revolts in Paris and Vienna, demonstrations which were held to protest at working and living conditions in Berlin were crushed by the Prussian cavalry, leaving 230 dead. The king made small concessions, paying lip service to the popular demand for press freedom and a constitutional monarchy. A year later, police controls had been tightened, press censorship resumed, and democratic meetings swarmed with government spies.

Prussia's success during the Franco-Prussian War (1870–1871) placed it at the head of a new united Germany. Under Kaiser Wilhelm I and Otto von Bismarck, Berlin became the *Reichshauptstadt* (capital of the empire). By 1880, amid the industrial expansion of the *Gründerzeit* (founding years), the city's population soared past the million mark. Berlin boomed as the center of Germany's machine industry and was a perfect market for mass-circulation newspapers and big department stores such as KaDeWe (Kaufhaus des Westens), founded in 1907.

After that philistine period of rapid growth, the city at last began to assume its place as Germany's cultural as well as political capital, with Berlin artists Max Liebermann, Lovis Corinth, and Max Slevogt challenging Munich's dominance of German painting. The Berlin Philharmonic asserted an international prestige, attracting Tchaikovsky, Strauss, and Grieg as guest composers, and in 1905, the great Viennese director Max Reinhardt arrived to head the Deutsches Theater.

Among its scientists, Robert Koch won a Nobel prize for his discovery of the *Tuberculosis bacillus*, and Max Planck headed the new Kaiser Wilhelm Society for the Advancement of Science (later named the Max-Planck-Institut), with Albert Einstein as director of the physics department.

War and Revolution

After years of opposition on social matters, Berliners solidly supported what proved to be the Hohenzollerns' last military gasp — World War I. At the start of the hostilities in August 1914, people gathered in thousands to cheer the Kaiser at the royal palace. The enthusiasm was short-lived.

Privations at home and the horrendous loss of life on the front turned popular feeling against the war. In 1916, Karl Liebknecht and Rosa Luxemburg formed the Spartacus League. Two years later, with Germany defeated and insurrections in Kiel, Munich, Hamburg, and Stuttgart, revolution broke out in Berlin. While the Social Democrats were proclaiming a new German Republic, Liebknecht took over the palace declaring the Republic socialist, with "supreme authority for the workers and soldiers."

Vehemently opposed to any Soviet-style revolution, Chancellor Friedrich Ebert and his Social Democrats outmanoeuvred the Spartacists. The ruthless defence minister Gustav Noske called in 4,000 *Freikorps* (right-wing storm-troopers) to smash the movement. They assassinated Liebknecht and Luxemburg on 15 January 1919. (A plaque on the Lützowufer marks the post where Rosa Luxemburg's body was fished out of the Landwehr canal.) Four days later, a new National Assembly was elected and the dominant Social Democrats moved the government to the safety of Weimar, 240 km (150 miles) southwest of Berlin, to draw up the constitution of the new Republic.

The Crazy Twenties

The use of the *Freikorps* to suppress the Spartacists was to haunt the Weimar Republic. In March 1920, the Kapp Putsch brought 5,000 of the storm-troopers into Berlin with an obscure civil servant, Wolfgang Kapp, installed as puppet chancellor. The coup lasted only five days, but set the tone for Germany's fragile experiment in parliamentary democracy. The swastika displayed on the helmets of the *Freikorps* was to reappear on the armbands of Hitler's storm-troopers, crushing all democracy in 1933.

The turbulent twenties gave Berlin a special place in the world's popular imagination. In 1920, the incorporation of 8 townships and some 60 suburban communities into the metropolis effectively doubled Berlin's population overnight to 4 million. Before democracy was extinguished in 1933, the city led a charmed life of exciting creativity that left its mark on the whole of European culture. Defeat in World War I had shattered the rigid certainties of Berlin's "Prussianness" and left the town open to radical adventures in social and artistic expression almost unimaginable in the older cultural capitals of Vienna, London and Paris.

Artists of the avant-garde intellectual movement known as Dada called for state prayers to be replaced by simultaneous poetry and regularization of sexual intercourse via a Central Dada Sex Office. Many years before the New York "happenings" of the 1960s, Berlin Dadaists were organizing races between a sewing machine and a typewriter, with writer Walter Mehring and artist Georg Grosz as jockeys.

In the meantime, nightclubs on Tauentzienstraße provided a combination of political satire and striptease, and sharp analysis of world affairs was accompanied by plenty of alcohol, cocaine, and sexual licence. The paintings of Otto Dix, Georg Grosz, and Max Beckmann were brutally realist, and the dissonance of the times was aptly captured by the atonal music composed by Arnold Schönberg and his pupil Alban Berg.

The conservative establishment winced when the Prussian Writers' Academy chose as its president Heinrich Mann, the elder brother of Thomas Mann, a violent critic of the German bourgeoisie and supporter of the Communist Party. His best-known novel, *Professor Unrat*, inspired Josef von Sternberg's *The Blue Angel*, the film that revealed the vocal talents of Marlene Dietrich.

Berlin showed its sense of the times with its mastery of film, the 20th-century art form. Fritz Lang, F.W. Murnau, G.W. Pabst, and Ernst Lubitsch were the leading directors of their generation. While Hollywood had considered cinema to be principally an industry of mass entertainment, the Berlin film-makers added a new perception of its artistic possibilities with *M*, *The Cabinet of Dr. Caligari*, *Lulu*, and *Nosferatu*. After seeing Fritz Lang's premonitory fable of human regimentation, *Metropolis*, Hitler wanted the master of the dark spectacle to make publicity films for him.

Berlin was going through a wild time, but the Versailles peace treaty had laid heavy burdens on the nation. At the start of the twenties, inflation had made a nonsense of the German currency, and political assassinations became routine, with the most significant of the victims being foreign minister Walther Rathenau, an enlightened democrat and Jew killed near the Grunewald forest. It was also the time of vicious street battles between Communists and Nazis exploiting the social disruptions of inflation and unemployment.

The Third Reich

Communist hostility towards the Social Democrats split the opposition to the Nazis. Hitler became Chancellor on 30 January 1933. Only a month later, on 27 February, the Reichstag went up in flames. Hitler used the fire as a pretext to eliminate Communist and all left-wing opposition from German political life. The Nazi reign of terror had begun.

Flames were the leitmotiv of the Third Reich in Berlin. On 10 May 1933, a procession brought thousands of students along Unter den Linden to the square before Humboldt University. They carried books, not to a lecture but to a bonfire on which were burned the works of Thomas Mann, Heinrich Mann, Stefan Zweig, Albert Einstein and Sigmund Freud, as well as Proust, Zola, Gide, H.G. Wells, and Jack London.

In 1936 a flame was brought from Athens to Berlin to inaugurate the Olympic Games, an attempt at Aryan propaganda which was soundly destroyed by black athlete Jesse Owens, who won four gold medals. In deference to foreign visitors, all anti-Semitic signs such as *Juden unerwünscht* (Jews not wanted) were removed from shops, hotels, and cafés. As soon as the foreigners had left town, the signs went up again.

Discrimination against Jews moved inexorably to the night of 9 November 1938, when synagogues and other Jewish-owned buildings were burned. In the midst of the smashed glass of the looted shops, German wit eased the discomfort by referring to the event as *Kristallnacht* (Crystal Night). Berlin's Jewish population, which stood at 170,000 in 1933, was reduced by emigration and extermination to around 6,000 by 1945.

World War II

In the autumn of 1938, Hitler was put out that Berliners did not share his enthusiasm for the cavalcade of troops driving through the city. The army was preparing its march into what used to be Czechoslovakia, but onlookers shared none of the fervour that had greeted military parades in 1914.

Their disquiet was shortly to be justified by the hail of bombs on the capital. The first attacks came in 1940 from the British in retaliation for the air raids on London. Attacks were stepped up after the German defeat at Stalingrad in 1943, with Anglo-American "carpet-bombing." The worst single raid was on 6 February 1945, when bombs wiped out 4 square km (1½ square miles) of the city center in one hour.

Hitler spent the last days of the war in his bunker at the Reich chancellery. As Soviet troops moved in to capture the city, he killed himself with a shot through the mouth.

The war ended with unconditional German surrender on 8 May 1945. In Berlin, the population was left to pick up the pieces — literally. Women formed groups of *Trümmerfrauen* (rubble women), with 60,000 of them passing the debris of war by hand to clear ground for rebuilding. Eventually there was sufficient rubble to create a few artificial mountains. One of them, Teufelsberg in the Grunewald, is big enough to ski on.

Division and Reunification

With the Soviet army already in place, American troops entered Berlin in 1945 on their national Independence Day, 4 July, followed by the British and French contingent. Four-power control of Berlin was agreed at Potsdam by Winston Churchill (replaced in mid-conference by Clement Attlee, his successor as Prime Minister), Harry Truman, and Joseph Stalin. The Soviet eastern sector covered just under half the city's area. The western sector was divided among the French in the north around Tegel Airport, the British mainly in the center from the Tiergarten to Spandau, and the Americans in the sprawling southwest corner from Kreuzberg out to the Grunewald and Wannsee.

Hard political realities soon developed from these administrative divisions, as the Allies found themselves confronted with Soviet efforts to incorporate the whole of Berlin into a new Communist-controlled German Democratic Republic. In the 1946 municipal elections — Berlin's first free vote since 1933, and its last until 1990 — the Social Democrats won a crushing victory over the Communists, prompting the Soviets to tighten their grip on the eastern sector. Understandably unhappy that West Berlin's capitalist presence in the middle of East Germany was having a subversive influence on the Communist ex-

The Potsdam Agreement at Cecilienhof sealed Berlin's fate in the aftermath of World War II.

periment, the Soviets and their East German allies began to restrict traffic from West Germany. In June 1948, all road, rail, and waterway routes to West Berlin were sealed off. From bases in Frankfurt, Hamburg, and Hanover, the Western Allies countered the blockade by airlifting into Berlin between 4,000 and 8,000 tons of food and other vital supplies every day for 11 months. The blockade finally ended in May 1949, and West Berlin became a *Land* linked administratively with, but thus far not politically incorporated into, the new Federal Republic of Germany. East Berlin was made capital of the fledgling German Democratic Republic.

Discontent with the living conditions in East Berlin first erupted into open revolt on 17 June 1953. Striking construction workers marched down Stalinallee (which was later renamed Karl-Marx-Allee) and mounted violent demonstrations against the government of Walter Ulbricht. They were protesting against the state demands for increased productivity while their standard of living continued to compare unfavourably with that of West Berlin. The revolt was crushed by Soviet tanks.

The Absent Monument

It's gone, but not forgotten. Fragments of *die Mauer* decorate mantlepieces and museums all over the world, but the city in which it was erected has done everything possible to obliterate its physical traces, if not its memory.

Masterminded by Ulbricht, the Berlin Wall grew from an improvised barbed-wire fence into a massive barrier 4 meters (13 feet) high, topped by concrete tubing to prevent easy handholds. Behind it, protected by an electrified fence, stretched a strip of sand 150 meters (490 feet) wide — a no-man's land equipped with watch-towers, patrol dogs, and searchlights. The most poignant stretch was in the district of Wedding, where Bernauerstraße ran one side in the east, the other in the west. After the border was closed in August 1961, people jumped to freedom from windows until workmen bricked them up.

Civilian escapes by tunnel, cars with hidden compartments, and other subterfuges, including by hot-air balloon, became as much a part of the Cold War legend as breakouts by prisoners of war were in World War II.

The so-called *Antifaschistischer Schutzwall* (anti-Fascist protective rampart) ended up simply as a gigantic quarry for rather squalid ornaments. No one who witnessed its construction and poisonous effect on daily life needs a souvenir.

By the end of the 1950s, the flow of refugees to the West had reached disastrous proportions for East Germany. Over 3 million citizens had fled the country, over half of them through Berlin, where border controls were only perfunctory. When Soviet leader Nikita Khrushchev decided to stop the haemorrhage, the country was losing millions of marks invested in the training of doctors, engineers, and other highly skilled workers seeking better wages in the West.

In the early hours of 13 August 1961, East German workers and soldiers began to erect the wall that would separate East and West Berlin and change the lives of several million people for nearly 30 years. The wall started out as barbed wire and road blocks, but refugees continued to make their way through the barriers, by swimming through sewers and canals and jumping from buildings and railway bridges. Soon, huge slabs of reinforced concrete and tank-traps formed a more impenetrable barrier. Crossing points were established for foreigners and for West Germans, but not for Berliners, until a tiny few were allowed across much later in the Cold War confrontation.

For the Western Alliance, the Wall made West Berlin an even more powerful propaganda symbol of democratic freedom. On his visit in 1963, U. S. President John F. Kennedy dramatically underlined the Western Allies' commitment to the city with his famous proclamation: "*Ich bin ein Berliner.*"

The erection of the Wall did significantly reduce the flow of refugees to a few isolated escapes, but the East German economy suffered even more from the assaults of massive mismanagement and high-level corruption. Erich Honecker's regime won international diplomatic recognition for East Berlin as its capital and, with gleaming hotels and skyscrapers, tried to give it a lustre to rival West Berlin. Beneath the surface, however, the drabness of daily life and lack of personal freedom continued to undermine any chance of popular support.

The final push which led to the collapse of the Berlin Wall came when an ecological campaign in Leipzig against nuclear weapons and industrial pollution grew into nationwide pressure for democratic freedom. In 1989, with thousands of East Germans fleeing to the West via Hungary, Czechoslovakia, and Poland, the country was swept up in the wave of eastern European revolutions unleashed by the reforms of Soviet leader Mikhail Gorbachev. His visit to East Berlin in October 1989 for the 40th anniversary of the German Democratic Republic left it clear that Soviet troops would no longer shore up its regime. The Berlin Wall was opened on 9 November 1989, and at midnight on 3 October 1990, a huge black, red, and gold national flag was hoisted at the Reichstag. East and West Berlin were again one.

The City Today

With a population in June 1990 of almost 3½ million, Berlin was far and away Germany's largest city and quickly declared the national capital again. International businessmen and bankers flocked into town, but Bonn, understandably, as well as many provincial politicians opposing too great a concentration of power in Berlin, were reluctant to see all the affairs of government desert the banks of the Rhine. Turning its back on its left-wing tradition, the city elected in 1990 a conservative mayor to cope with the enormous day-to-day problems in housing, employment, and transport arising from reunification.

On 20 June 1991, the city's role at the hub of German life was assured when the Bundestag voted by a slim majority to restore Berlin as the seat of government. The transfer is scheduled to be completed by the year 2000, and the 21st century will no doubt see Germany playing a determining role in the shaping of Europe.

Historical Landmarks

Beginnings

1237-44	First record of Cölln and Berlin.
1307	The two townships are consolidated as one city.
1486	Residence of the Elector of Brandenburg.

Reformation

1539	Berliners force Joachim II to turn Protestant.
1618-48	Thirty Years War and plague halve population to barely 5,000.
1696-1700	Arts and science academies founded.

Rise of Prussia

1740-86	Frederick the Great ascends to the throne.
1791	Brandenburg Gate completed.
1806-8	Napoleon occupies Berlin.
1848	Democratic revolt crushed.

Capital of Germany

1871	Bismarck imposes Berlin as capital of Germany.
1918	November Revolution; new Republic proclaimed at the Reichstag.
1933	Hitler imposes dictatorship after Reichstag fire.
1936	Berlin hosts XI Olympic Games.
1938-9	November: *Kristallnacht* pogrom.
1939-45	World War II reduces population from 4.3 million to 2.8 million.

Division and Unification

1945	Berlin is divided and controlled by the four Powers of the Western Allies.
1953	17 June: Soviet tanks crush East Berlin uprising.
1961	Construction of the Berlin Wall.
1989	East German regime toppled; Berlin Wall opened on 9 November.
1990	Reunited German capital elects first unified Berlin parliament in over 40 years.
1991	20 June: Berlin again becomes the seat of government.

WHERE TO GO

You'll need to plan carefully for a thorough exploration of Berlin—with a total area of 880 square km (340 square miles) it is more than eight times the size of Paris. Since the reorganization of the municipal transport system, virtually the whole of the city is accessible via underground (*U-Bahn*), overhead (*S-Bahn*) railways, bus or tram. You should have no difficulty in reaching the outlying areas, including Spandau, the museums in Dahlem, the parks and lakes in the Grunewald, and the summer palaces in Potsdam, by public transport. Busy traffic and the inevitable parking problems make car hire a less attractive, and quite unnecessary, option.

A good orientation exercise is to start with an organized sightseeing tour—by bus, for instance, departing from the eastern end of the Kurfürstendamm. Cruises on the Landwehrkanal or Spree and Havel rivers offer a more leisurely way of taking in areas of eastern and western Berlin that are not normally covered by the tour buses. A more economical tour covering some of the city's famous monuments is offered by the bus 100, which shuttles at regular intervals between Bahnhof Zoo and Alexanderplatz, following a route which goes down Unter den Linden, through the Brandenburg Gate and past the Reichstag.

Signs:
Ankunft-**arrival**
Abflug/Abfahrt-**departure**
Raucher-**Smoker**
Nichtraucher-**Nonsmoker**

The area on and around the Kurfürstendamm is probably the best place to begin, as it's very well served by information centers and other tourist facilities, Your first port of call should be the **Berlin Tourist Office** which can be found at the Budapester Straße side of the Europa-Center and is open every day; the helpful, multilingual staff will assist you with maps, leaflets, and other useful information.

AROUND KURFÜRSTENDAMM

Berlin's main thoroughfare, literally "Prince Elector's Embankment," is known to Berliners as the **Ku'damm**. It extends for 3½ km (about 2 miles) through the center of the city, forming a triangular area enclosed by Lietzenburger Straße, Hardenbergstraße, Leibnizstraße, and Tauentzienstraße. Here you'll find most of the major shops, cafés, restaurants, theaters, cinemas, and art galleries, as well as no-frills fast-food stands, and the inevitable souvenir-sellers.

Impressed by the prolongation of the Champs-Elysées in Paris to the Bois de Boulogne, Bismarck wanted to extend the Ku'damm out as far as the Grunewald forest. However, such imperial pretentions were never realized, and finally the

Symbol of a divided city—
the Berlin sculpture at the far end of Kurfürstendamm.

avenue linked Kaiser Wilhelm Memorial Church to nothing grander than the Halensee railway station.

In the center of **Tauentzienstraße**, notice the intertwined steel tubes of the *Berlin* sculpture, which were designed for the city's 750th anniversary in 1987. The two halves are tantalizingly close to each other, yet fail to touch, poignantly symbolizing the divided city.

At the far end of Tauentzienstraße, **Wittenbergplatz** is a large, populous square and contains one of Berlin's many memorials; a sign outside the U-Bahn station which reminds passers-by of the Nazi concentration camps. The station itself is a beautifully restored Art Deco delight with lovely wooden ticket booths, period posters, and a central standing clock.

The Essentials

For those either on a brief visit to Berlin or who want to see the main sights before making a thorough tour of the town, here are the principal highlights, in alphabetical order:

More than just a department store, **KaDeWe**, located on the edge of Wittenbergplatz, has achieved the status of a monument. Founded in 1907, Kaufhaus des Westens (Department Store of the West) now claims to be the third largest department store in the world. The food emporium on the sixth floor is extraordinary. Here, any gourmet globetrotters can perch on a bar stool and sample not only food from all over Germany but also Chinese, Japanese, Russian, French, and Swiss cuisine. One floor up, the Wintergarten is a vast food court in the glass-roofed atri-

*KaDeWe — more than a department store:
a glittering monument to consumerism.*

um where shoppers can help themselves to less exotic, but equally tasty fare.

Breitscheidplatz is the big pedestrianized area at the base of the Europa-Center and a busy gathering place for shoppers and sightseers during the day. In the center of the square is Joachim Schmettau's granite **Weltkugelbrunnen** (or Fountain of the World), which locals have gaily christened the "aquatic dumpling." The split globe represents the old East-West division.

Soaring above it is another powerful symbol of the city, the **Kaiser-Wilhelm-Gedächtniskirche**. The 1943 bombing, combined with artillery fire at the end of the war, left the tower with the broken stump of its spire—63 meters (206 feet) compared with its original 113 meters (370 feet)—as a monumental ruin recalling the city's destruction. Flanking it, a modern octagonal church to the east and a chapel and hexagonal tower to the west represent the city's post-war rebirth. Stained glass from Chartres set in walls of moulded concrete casts a mysterious bluish glow over the Ku'damm at night.

Built between 1891–1895 to honour Wilhelm I, the remains of this neo-Romanesque church constitute a memorial hall to celebrate the Hohenzollerns' pious monarchism. A mosaic representing Christ the King is set above friezes and reliefs of Prussian monarchs from Friedrich I (1415–1440) to the last crown prince, Friedrich Wilhelm, who died in 1951. On one wall, Wilhelm I confers with Chancellor Bismarck and Field Marshals Moltke and Roon. With their taste for irreverent nicknames, Berliners have deflated the monuments' imperial or pacifist intentions by dubbing the original church the "broken tooth" and the two main additions the "lipstick" and "powder compact."

Beyond the church is the enormous **Europa-Center,** between Tauentzienstraße and Budapester Straße. The center was built in the 1960s and houses scores of shops, restaurants, a hotel, and a casino amidst artificial ponds and waterfalls. The structure inside the building with neon-yellow liquid bubbling away in glass tubes is not a large-scale chemistry set but a rather ingenious thermal clock.

Berlin's magnificent City Center Zoo is the second largest zoo in the world.

As zoos go—and many would like to see them go—the **Zoo**, entrance on Budapester Straße, has one of the most varied collections of animals in Europe. Beyond the colourful pagoda-arched **Elefantentor** (Elephant Gate) are 35 hectares (86 acres) of parkland where you will be able to observe Indian and African elephants, giant pandas from China, and the rare single-horned rhinoceros from India.

Sooner or later, everybody comes to promenade along the Ku'damm, and a suitable vantage point from which to survey them is **Café Kranzler**, a Berlin institution at the corner of Joachimstaler Straße. It's now decidedly bourgeois, although the original Kranzler at the west end of Unter den Linden between Friedrichstraße and the Brandenburg Gate was a hotbed of radical intellectuals in 1848 (see page 17).

The avenue lost almost all the Jugendstil architecture of its Wilhelminian heyday during World War II, but a vestige can be seen in the elegant **Café Möhring** just across the road. Note, too, the façade of number 52, a handsome Art Deco apartment building. Otherwise the street is resolutely modern—gleaming glass, steel, and an occasional touch of marble—but still a magnet for fashionable shopping.

Off the Ku'damm at Fasanenstraße 79 you will find the **Jüdisches Gemeindezentrum** (Jewish Community Center). Framing the entrance is the domed portal from the synagogue which was burned during the fateful *Kristallnacht* of 1938 (see page 21). The modern building serves as a cultural center for the 15,000 Jews still living in Berlin today—in 1933 they numbered some 170,000. The Noah's Ark restaurant inside the Community Center serves up substantial kosher fare as well as holding a marvellous Tuesday night buffet.

It's worth exploring some of the other side streets off the Ku'damm. As well as Fasanenstraße, you will discover many other elegant tree-lined boulevards studded with beautiful, balconied villas, antique shops, art galleries, and exclusive designer boutiques. A little to the north, fashionable **Savignyplatz** provides a focus for first-class art and architecture bookshops and art galleries, located in the arches beneath the overhead S-Bahn railway line. Here you will find an abundance of literary cafés, bistros, and bars, with plenty of outside seating, particularly along Grolmanstraße and Mommsenstraße.

TIERGARTEN AREA

Despite its name, the **Tiergarten** (literally "animal garden") is not another zoo. For the Hohenzollern princes, it was a forest for hunting deer and wild boar. After Frederick the Great cut down the woods to create a formal French garden for his brother August Ferdinand, it was replanted with trees in the 19th century and transformed into a landscaped park. Following World War II the Berliners stripped away the trees again—for fuel. Everything you will see here today has been planted since 1950, among pleasant ponds, cafés, and various monuments.

The **Englischer Garten** (beside Altonaer Straße), financed by British donations, was laid out by the Shropshire Horticultural Society, and forms part of the grounds of

The elegant Schloß Bellevue in the Tiergarten is the German president's official residence.

Schloß Bellevue, a neo-classical style palace that was for years the official residence of the German President when he was in Berlin, but with the government's move to Berlin is being converted into the official government guest house— the President is taking up permanent residence in the Crown Prince's Palace on Unter den Linden.

On the north-west side of the Tiergarten is the **Hansaviertel**, a chic, though slightly dated, residential neighbourhood rebuilt by architects for the International Building Exhibition of 1957. Amongst the winners were Bauhaus founder Walter Gropius (Händelallee 1-9), the Brazilian Oscar Niemeyer (Altonaer Straße 4-14), and Alvar Aalto from Finland (Klopstockstraße 30). Their names are inscribed along with the locations of their projects on a map on Klopstockstraße.

The **Berlin-Pavillon** (Straße des 17. Juni), which stands on the edge of the Tiergarten, was built at the same time as the Hansaviertel. The white pavilion is an airy, single-storey building, now used for temporary exhibitions on town planning, modern architecture, and ecology. Nearby, at Hanseatenweg 10, the **Akademie der Künste** (Arts Academy) holds concerts, plays, and exhibitions of avant-garde art.

At the center of the park, on the circle of the Großer Stern, the soaring **Siegessäule** (Victory Column) is an unabashed monument dedicated to Prussian militarism. It was completed in 1873, two years after the victory over the French, and also commemorates successes against Denmark and Austria in 1864 and 1866 respectively. A climb of around 285 steps takes you to the top of the 67 meters (220 feet) column for a breathtaking view over the city from beneath the gilded bronze statue of Winged Victory.

On the north side of the Großer Stern are monuments honouring the architects of that first unification, the Field Marshals Moltke and Roon, and Chancellor Bismarck.

Follow the River Spree to the east along Spreeweg until you reach the **Kongreßhalle**, built by the Americans as their country's contribution to the 1957 International Building Exhibition. Officially renamed **Haus der Kulturen der Welt** (House of World Cultures), the striking design, with its curved concrete roof, (which was rebuilt after collapsing in 1980) led Berliners to dub the building the "pregnant oyster." The vast space inside is used for temporary exhibitions on global cultures and non-European avant-garde art, and there's also a conference room, restaurant, café, and theater. In front of the building, the pond features a sculpture in bronze by the ubiquitous Henry Moore, and is attractively illuminated at night. An austere black structure stands on the corner of Große Querallee near the Kongreßhalle. Built in 1987, the 42 meter-(138 foot-) tall tower contains a 68-bell **carillon**, played by hand on a special keyboard, which chimes daily at noon and six.

☞ The Reichstag

A few minutes' walk from the Kongreßhalle you'll find the **Reichstag** building, which is undergoing extensive renovations that include a new glass dome. The parliamentary home of Wilhelminian and Weimar Germany displays the proud dedication *Dem deutschen Volke* (To the German People) on a neoclassical façade built in 1894 by Paul Wallot. This appeal to patriotism and democracy, set above six Corinthian columns, outlasted the burning in 1933 and the bombs of World War II, and is given renewed significance as Berlin resumes its former role as the seat of government of a unified Germany. The first session of a united German parliament was held here in October 1990, and the national government is scheduled to complete its transfer from Bonn by the year 2000.

South of the Siegessäule, the stylized industrial curves of the **Bauhaus-Archiv** (see page 71) on the Landwehr canal

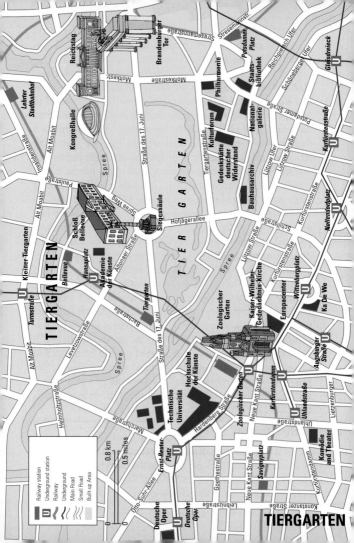

TIERGARTEN

were designed by Walter Gropius, founder of the hugely influential Bauhaus school of architecture, art and design.

Note Emil Fahrenkamp's gracefully curved, travertine-clad **Bewag Building** on the corner of Stauffenbergstraße and Reichpietschufer. It was built originally for Shell Oil in 1932, and now serves as the head office of the Berlin electric company. The **Gedenkstätte Deutscher Widerstand** is a memorial to German resistance against Fascism within the *Bendlerblock*, the former German military headquarters. A bronze statue depicting a young man with bound hands stands in the courtyard where Graf von Stauffenberg and other army officers who conspired to blow up Hitler on 20 July 1944 were shot. An excellent free exhibition in the historical rooms of the building where the attempted coup was planned, contains more than 5,000 photographs and historical documents charting the tragic course of resistance.

At the corner of Potsdamer Straße, Bauhaus master Mies van der Rohe's design for the **Neue Nationalgalerie** of 20th-century art (see page 72) is a square, glass-wall structure with a vast, black steel roof supported by eight massive steel columns. This work of characteristic elegant simplicity was completed in 1968, a year before the architect's death. It stands on a rather windswept, raised granite platform that serves as a sculpture court for huge outdoor pieces like Henry Moore's *Archer*, as well as a providing a playground for skate-boarders. A new wing housing European paintings from the 14th through 18th centuries opens in 1998.

 ## Kulturforum

Beyond the Nationalgalerie, in dignified isolation, is the fine-steepled neo-Romanesque **St. Matthäiskirche**, built in the Italian Renaissance style in 1846 by August Stüler. It is the only pre-war building hereabouts to survive Albert Speer's redesign of Berlin, and forms the nucleus about which the concert halls and the museums (including the Neue Nationalgalerie) of the city's Cultural Forum are clustered. (See pages TK for a description of the museums' contents.)

The prints and watercolours comprising the **Kupferstichkabinett** (Engravings Collection) were transferred from Museumsinsel and Dahlem to a new home in Matthäiskirchplatz in mid-1993.

Eclipsed by the sober international style imposed by the Bauhaus in the 1920s—of which the Neue Nationalgalerie is a prime example—architect Hans Scharoun was at last able to indulge his taste for Expressionistic free-form structures. His first design, the controversial ochre and gold **Philharmonie**, owes its tent-like shape to the demands of the concert hall's acoustics and sight-lines. The home of the Berlin Philharmonic Orchestra was designed from the inside out, from the orchestra to the walls and roof. Viewed from across Tiergartenstraße, the nearby **Musikinstrumentenmuseum** is reminiscent of an open card index file and hous-

The Reichstag — a potent symbol of democracy and home to the united German parliament.

es an extensive collection of instruments from the 16th century to the present.

Opposite the Philharmonie on Matthäiskirchplatz stands The **Kunstgewerbemuseum** (Arts and Crafts Museum). It was completed in 1985 and is a rather confusing labyrinth of red brick and white granite, but it is worth a visit for its superb collection of medieval jewellery. The nearby **Staatsbibliothek** (State Library), Potsdamer Straße 33, was also designed by Scharoun. Despite its formidable dimensions, the library is a model of peace and harmony. A quite ingenious network of staircases leads to multi-level reading rooms and easily accessible stacks. It's one of the largest modern library buildings in Europe, and regularly holds documentary and photographic exhibitions as well as concerts.

Potsdamer Platz

Reduced by war and the Wall to a bleak no-man's-land, the square that was at one time the busiest in Europe shows signs of coming back to life. The area is now the target of feverish urban planning with projects such as prestigious office buildings and commercial centers above ground, and extensions to rail networks below. A mound on the wasteland that lies between Pariser Platz and Potsdamer Platz marks the site of what's left of the Führerbunker, where Hitler took his own life (see page 22).

The **Martin-Gropius-Bau**, surrounded by weeds and rubble, is situated nearby at Stresemann Straße 110, It was originally built between 1877 and 1881 by Martin Gropius, (great-uncle of the Bauhaus's Walter Gropius) with the help of Heino Schmieden, as an arts and crafts museum (the collection is now divided between the Kunstgewerbemuseums at Schloß Köpenick and in the Kulturforum). The lavish red and gold building is a spacious exhibition site housing in and around its skylighted inner courtyard area collections of the **Berlinische Galerie**, the **Werkbund-Archiv,** and the **Jewish Museum** (see page 70).

The piece of land which lies adjacent to the Martin-Gropius-Bau is the site of Prinz-Albrecht-Straße 8, the former School of Applied Arts and Design, which served as the headquarters of the SS, Gestapo, and other Nazi institutions. Excavations in 1987 revealed the cellars where thousands of victims were imprisoned and tortured. A low, white building constructed above the underground quarters of the SS guards houses the **Topographie des Terrors**, a (free) exhibition of photographs and documents which movingly illustrates the lives of those who resisted the Nazi terror.

Further along at Askanischer Platz is the sad but graceful arcaded ruin of **Anhalter Bahnhof**. By an irony of latterday history, the old railway station was the work of Franz Schwechten, the architect who created the Kaiser Wilhelm Memorial Church, that other noble ruin (see page 31). Today, the wasteland left by the deserted goods yards has become a biotope supporting shrubs and trees, such as the *Robinia* locust tree, that are foreign to this northern-European region. Here you will also find the entrance to the **Deutsches Technikmuseum Berlin (German Technology Museum)**, (page 70).

Last Train to Safety

The Anhalter Bahnhof's elegant neo-Renaissance façade is a nicely preserved reminder of what was once Berlin's most glamorous railway station, linking the city to Europe's other great capitals. Its west-bound platform staged the tragic last act of the Weimar Republic. Soon after Hitler became Chancellor, Berlin's most gifted artists and intellectuals — among them Heinrich Mann, Bertolt Brecht, Kurt Weill, Georg Grosz, Albert Einstein — gathered here, their bags packed for exile.

MITTE

The area east of the Brandenburg Gate known as **Mitte** (Middle) is the historic center of Berlin, and was at one time the center of the capital of the German Democratic Republic. The city's most important museums, theaters, government buildings, and churches were constructed here between the 18th and 20th centuries. Many buildings, including the Friedrichswerdersche Kirche (now home to the Schinkel-Museum, see page 78) and Schinkel's Altes Museum (Old Museum) (see page 74), were carefully restored by East Germany after air-raid bombing of World War II, and several quarters were rebuilt in the Old Berlin style, notably Gendarmenmarkt (formerly Platz der Akademie) and Museumsinsel, (see page 73).

Today, the area's principal avenue, **Unter den Linden**, is regaining its former importance as the main focus of the capital's cultural and political life, while nearby Friedrichstraße is once again becoming a fashionable shopping artery, with the opening of several new shopping complexes. When you talk to people here, however, it's worth bearing in mind that eastern Berlin did not turn into a bastion of anti-Communism overnight. Although the city voted in a conservative mayor in December 1990, the successor party to the Communists did exceptionally well in the old eastern boroughs, still a solid left-wing stronghold.

Brandenburg Gate

This formidable symbol of the united city appears at last to be realizing the vision of Johann Gottfried Schadow, the sculptor who crowned the Brandenburg Gate with the Quadriga, a copper statue of Winged Victory in her four-horse chariot. Schadow had wanted the gate to be known as the *Friedenstor* (Gate of Peace), in keeping with the relief of the *Procession of Peace* that he himself had sculpted beneath Victory's simple chariot.

The gate itself, designed by Carl Gotthard Langhans, was built between 1789 and 1791. With two rows of six Doric columns forming the gateway proper, it was inspired by the Propylaeum gatehouse leading to the Parthenon in Athens. (To go the whole hog, Hitler had even planned to hoist the gate onto an artificial hill, in an attempt to create a mini-Acropolis.) Forming part of the city wall, the gate was intended by the more pragmatic Prussians not so much as a triumphal arch as an imposing tollgate for collecting duties.

The gate was left isolated in no-man's land when the Wall went up, and subsequently became the scene of quite ecstatic celebrations when it came down, though now you would scarcely believe it as Berliners cross nonchalantly from east to west through Brandenburg's mighty central arch.

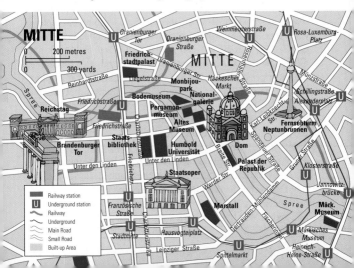

*The majestic Brandenburg Gate, through which
all Berliners are now free to pass.*

☞ Unter den Linden

Sweeping eastwards from the gate, this grand 61 meters
(200-foot-) wide avenue, literally named "Beneath the Linden Trees," was Berlin's showcase boulevard. Frederick the
Great saw it as the center of his royal capital, and it became
the most prestigious address in town. Some of its splendour
fell victim to 19th-century building speculation, but the avenue remained fashionable until the bombs of World War II
reduced it to rubble. Now the trees have been replanted and
the most important buildings restored.

Its western end is dominated by the Russian Federation
Embassy, on the right as you come from Brandenburg Gate,
East of Charlottenstraße, beyond the patched, dark stone of
the **Deutsche Staatsbibliothek** (German State Library),
built between 1903 and 1914 but damaged during the Second World War II, is Frederick the Great's architectural com-

plex known as "Forum Fridericianum." An imposing statue of the monarch on horseback (1851), the work of Christian Daniel Rauch, stands in the avenue's central strip.

To recreate the cultural climate that his grandfather had brought to Berlin during the 17th century, the king commissioned a new building to house the Royal Academy, a library, an opera house, and a palace for his brother, Prince Heinrich. The result was Heinrich's palace (1748), which is now beautifully restored, and forms part of **Humboldt Universität**. Founded in 1810 by brothers Alexander and Wilhelm Humboldt, the institution counted among its professors and students Hegel, Engels, Marx, and Einstein, as well as the Grimm brothers. Opposite its rather severe classicism is the curving baroque façade of the **Alte Bibliothek** (Old Library). It stands beside the open square named **Bebelplatz** (formerly Opernplatz) which was the scene of book-burning by Nazi students in 1933.

Across Bebelplatz you will find the grand Palladian-style **Deutsche Staatsoper** (German State Opera) designed in 1742 by Knobelsdorff, Frederick the Great's favourite architect. To the east of the square, the **Operncafé** is housed in the Prinzessinnenpalais, the Prussian princesses' baroque town house. Its open-air terrace is one of the most popular places to meet in the eastern part of Berlin, while inside there are four more elegant cafés and restaurants to be enjoyed.

Beside the university, the old Prussian army guardhouse, the Neue Wache (New Guardhouse), known as the **Mahnmal**, was

> Signs:
> *Eingang*-entrance
> *Ausgang/Ausfahrt*-exit

Karl Friedrich Schinkel's first important neo-classical design, completed in 1818. It was rebuilt at the end of World War II as a memorial to victims of Fascism and militarism,

This thrilling bronze sculpure of a lion slayer stands outside the Altes Museum.

and an enlargement of a Käthe Kollwitz *Pietà* by Harald Haackehas recently been installed.

Next door is the handsome, baroque **Zeughaus**, once arsenal for the Prussian Army, as the sculpted suits of armour testify along the roof. At present, part of the **Museum für Deutsche Geschichte** (German History Museum) can be found there, although it is destined for use by the government when the move to Berlin is finalized. The artist Andreas Schlüter provided the military sculpture, but was able to assert his pacifist views with poignant sculpted masks of dying warriors (1696) in the inner courtyard named after him, the **Schlüterhof**.

To the south of the Staatsoper on the corner of the square is **St. Hedwigs-Kathedrale**, from 1747, a huge, domed structure built for the Catholics incorporated into Protestant Prussia by Frederick's conquest of Polish Silesia.

The celebrated architectural ensemble south of Unter den Linden on the Gendarmenmarkt has been almost completely restored after near total destruction during World War II. The square is bordered by bookshops and cafés set in delightful arcades. The imposing **Schiller-Denkmal** (1868), a monument sculpted in Carrara marble, surrounds the writer with the muses of philosophy, poetry, drama, and history.

It stands in front of Schinkel's Ionic-porticoed **Schauspielhaus** (Playhouse), which is now a concert hall. The edifice links two identical churches, the **Französischer Dom** (or French Cathedral) to the north, built for the immigrant Huguenots, and the **Deutscher Dom** (German Cathedral) to the south. Both were built in the early 18th century. The twin domes were added in 1785.

Step inside the Französischer Dom to visit the Huguenot museum, or look up the stairwell to the Glockenspiel—a dizzying 48 meter

Music lovers flock to another outstanding performance at the German State Opera.

(159 feet) above. The **Turmstuben** restaurant on the fourth floor is the place to calm your shattered nerves. The Deutscher Dom now houses a fascinating exhibition, *Fragen an die deutsche Geschichte* (German History Under Question), which was previously in the Reichstag. This frank examination of Germany's social and political history cleverly combines documents, photographs, and radio broadcasts to chronicle the rise of Fascism and the development of democracy. The descriptive panels are all in German, but tape

Unter den Linden's Operncafé rivals the best the west has to offer and is perfect for outdoor rendezvous overlooking the Spree.

guides and information booklets are available in English and French.

Oranienburger Straße

On the north side of the River Spree, Oranienburger Straße is the heart of the old Jewish quarter. In the 1920s, a diverse community of Jewish professionals and Bohemian artists and writers lived, worked, and thrived here. After the devastation of the war and the grim sterility of its aftermath, the area is regaining its former vibrancy, with cultural centers and Jewish restaurants rubbing shoulders with off-beat cafés and alternative art venues beneath the magnificent black and gold-leafed dome of the **Neue Synagogue**. The biggest synagogue in Germany, designed by Eduard Knoblauch and completed in 1866, it was gutted during the anti-Semitic attacks of *Kristallnacht* on 9 November 1938 (see page 21) and then later destroyed by Allied bombing. Its façade has now been beautifully restored, and a new center of Jewish studies, Centrum Judaicum, has opened inside the building, with exhibits and retrospectives of Jewish artists, lectures, and tours on Jewish history.

Karl-Liebknecht-Straße

Linking Unter den Linden to Karl-Liebknecht-Straße is the 19th century **Schloßbrücke** (Palace Bridge), designed by Schinkel in 1820–1824, and decorated with fierce warriors and victory goddesses. Beyond the bridge, look left to the imposing neo-classical façade of the **Altes Museum** at the far end of the **Lustgarten** (Pleasure Garden), which forms a grand entrance to **Museumsinsel**, the site of eastern Berlin's most important museums (see pages 73–78). On the opposite side of the Lustgarten, the rather desolate area formerly known as Marx-Engels-Platz was a focus of Communist May Day military parades and rallies. The war-damaged Stadtschloß (City Palace) of the Hohenzollerns once stood here. However, in 1950 Walter Ulbricht decided to raze it as symbolizing German imperialism, despite protests from art historians that it was the city's outstanding baroque building. (You can see a model of the palace in the historical apartments at Schloß Charlottenburg, see page 53.)

The palace balcony from which Spartacist leader Karl Liebknecht proclaimed his doomed "Socialist Republic" in 1918 was added to the front of the **Staatsrat** (Council of State) building on the east side of the square, while the monstrous bronze, glass, and steel Palast der Republik, once, not so very long ago, the seat of East Germany's parliament, replaced what remained of the royal residence. Recent budget cuts have postponed the demolition of the Palast, and there is a movement afoot to preserve it as a historic monument.

On the opposite side, the exterior of Kaiser Wilhelm II's **Berliner Dom** has been completely restored, and its interior beautifully renovated, after sustaining heavy bomb damage during the Second World War. The cathedral acts as a place of worship as well as a museum, and has a crypt containing 95 Hohenzollern sarcophagi.

Continue along Karl-Liebknecht-Straße as far as the **Marienkirche** (13th century) on Neuer Markt, a haven of sober Gothic simplicity amidst the prevailing bombast. Inside, see Schlüter's baroque marble pulpit (1703) and a late-Gothic fresco of the *Dance of Death* (1484) in the tower hall.

The neo-Renaissance Berliner Rathaus, also known as the **Rotes Rathaus** (Red Town Hall), owes its nickname to its red clinker masonry, not its ideology. Built between 1861 and 1869, it is now the seat of the city's governing mayor, and is decorated with an interesting terracotta frieze chronicling the history of Berlin up to the time of the building's construction.

Beyond the huge **Neptunbrunnen** (Neptune's Fountain), a rather elaborate affair decorated with four figures representing the rivers Rhine, Elbe, Oder, and Weichsel, you can hardly miss the **Fernsehturm** (Television Tower) rising up above Alexanderplatz. It was built in 1969, and at 365 meters (1,197 feet) absolutely dwarfs western Berlin's Funkturm (see pages 56–57), which was the object of the exercise. Not for the faint-hearted, an observation deck at 207 meters (679 feet) affords an excellent view over the city, while the revolving restaurant provides refreshment.

Alexanderplatz

"**Alex**," as the huge square is known, was once the undisputed heart of pre-war Berlin, and its vibrancy was celebrated in Alfred Döblin's great 1929 novel *Berlin Alexanderplatz*, later filmed by Rainer Werner Fassbinder. Today the square is a rather bleak and desolate place with a fountain and a circular World Clock, surrounded by grim, graffiti-ridden Communist architecture. However, plans are afoot to knock down and rebuild part of the area and restore some of the square's former vitality.

The crumbling façades of apartments, hotels, and new-ly established bargain basement shops line **Karl-Marx-Allee** leading south east from Alex. Walk up and down it if only to re-mind yourself what soul-less buildings Stalinist architects could produce. Until 1961 the street was known as Stalin-Allee, al-though it's highly probable that its name will be changed again in the near future.

The Berliner Dom is one of many splendid buildings to undergo extensive post-war restoration.

To the north of Alexanderplatz, behind the Volksbühne theater, **Schönhauser Allee** is one of the most characteristic avenues of Old Berlin leading to the center of **Prenzlauer Berg**, the working-class quarter. Four- and five-storey tenement blocks are interspersed with decaying mansions in the very heart of eastern Berlin's *Alternativen* community. On **Husemannstraße**, a number of buildings from the age of Kaiser Wilhelm II have been pleasingly restored.

Nikolaiviertel

South of the Rotes Rathaus, the neighbourhood of Nikolai was restored for Berlin's 750th anniversary celebrations in 1987, as a "clean" example of Old Berlin. The site of Berlin's earliest settlement, it clusters around the city's oldest parish church, the twin-steepled Gothic-style **Nikolaikirche**. The church was built in 1230 and now forms part of the **Märkisches Museum** (see page 77), devoted to the city's history. Among the buildings resurrected here is the **Gaststätte zum Nußbaum**, the favourite tavern of cartoonist Heinrich Zille. The **Knoblauchhaus**, at Poststraße 23, is an elegant house rebuilt in neo-classi-

> Most public telephones don't use coins anymore but a telephone card *(Telefonkarte)*.

cal style in 1835 and containing some fine Biedermeier furniture. More stately is the reconstructed **Ephraimpalais**, Poststraße 16, a rococo mansion built for Friedrich II's financier Veitel Heine Ephraim in 1765. Besides providing a delightful setting for chamber-music recitals, it is also used for exhibitions of 18th- and 19th-century art and Berlin history.

Architects of Berlin

ANDREAS SCHLÜTER (1664-1714). Berlin's foremost baroque architect, responsible for giving the city much of its royal appearance. Look for the 21 masks of dying soldiers in the Zeughaus courtyard (Schlüterhof) in Unter den Linden, and the equestrian statue of Frederick the Great outside Schloß Charlottenburg.

GEORG WENZELAUS VON KNOBELSDORFF (1699-1753). Frederick the Great's favourite architect. Included among his contributions are St. Hedwig's-Kathedrale and the Deutsche Staatsoper on Unter den Linden; the new wing at Schloß Charlottenburg; and the splendidly rococo Schloß Sanssouci in Potsdam.

KARL FRIEDRICH SCHINKEL (1781-1841). Berlin's most gifted and prolific neo-classical architect. His other talents were landscape painting and stage design. Works include the Neue Wache and the Altes Museum in and around Unter den Linden; the Schauspielhaus at Gendarmenmarkt; and the neo-Gothic war memorial in Viktoria Park, Kreuzberg.

SCHLOSS CHARLOTTENBURG

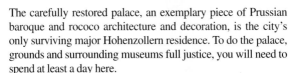

The carefully restored palace, an exemplary piece of Prussian baroque and rococo architecture and decoration, is the city's only surviving major Hohenzollern residence. To do the palace, grounds and surrounding museums full justice, you will need to spend at least a day here.

Badly damaged in a World War II air raid, Schloß Charlottenburg became the target of extensive post-war reconstruction, and now functions as a major museum complex. The **Galerie der Romantik** (Gallery of Romantic Art) and the **Museum für Vor- und Frühgeschichte** (Museum of Primeval and Early History) are housed in the east and west wings respectively, while the **Haus der Zeitgenössischen Kunst** (a collection of contemporary art) and the **Ägyptisches Museum** (Egyptian Museum) are in identical guardhouses opposite the palace. You will find the **Bröhan-Museum** (dedicated to Art Deco and Art Nouveau) in a former infantry barracks opposite the Egyptian museum. A detailed description of each museum is given on pages 65–67.

Schloß Charlottenburg was conceived as a summer retreat for the future Queen Sophie Charlotte in the 1690s, when the site beside the River Spree, west of the Tiergarten, lay well outside the city limits. It was a small palace—scarcely one-fifth of the huge structure you see today—and only with the addition of a majestic domed tower (with the goddess Fortune as its weathervane), the Orangerie to the west and a new east wing, did it become big enough for Frederick the Great. If he ever had to leave his beloved Potsdam, this was where he came.

In the palace courtyard you will find an **equestrian statue** of the Great Elector Friedrich Wilhelm, designed by Andreas Schlüter in 1697. One of many art works lost in World War II, it was finally recovered from Tegel Lake in 1949, where it

Queen Sophie Charlotte's palace, once a rural retreat, is now an enchanting place for visitors to explore.

had sunk with the barge that was taking it to safety.

To try and recapture the interior's rather gracious rococo atmosphere, furniture, and decorations from other Prussian palaces built in the 18th-century have been used to replace what was destroyed here during World War II. Visitors are free to roam at will through the Hohenzollerns' ornate world, except for Friedrich I's and Sophie Charlotte's apartments in the **Neringbau** and **Eosanderbau**, for which there are regular guided tours (in German only). Be sure to arrive early to avoid the queues.

In the **Gobelinzimmer**, notice the fine 18th-century tapestries by Charles Vigne. The rays of light on the ceiling of the **Audienzzimmer** (Reception Room) and bright yellow damask walls in the **Schlafzimmer** (bedroom) imitate the motif of the Sun King, Louis XIV, the Prussian rulers' hero. Chinoiserie is the dominating feature of the opulent **Porzellankabinett**, filled to the ceiling with hundreds of pieces of Chinese and Japanese porcelain. The relatively sober **Japanische Kammer** contains some prized lacquered cabinets and tables. The tapestries depict landscapes of China, in spite of the chamber's name. Chamber music recitals can be heard in the **Eichengalerie** (Oak Gallery) and the **Eosander-Kapelle** (chapel) which boasts an extravagant rococo decor that makes it more a theater than place of worship.

Designed for Frederick the Great by Georg von Knobelsdorff, the **Neuer Flügel** (new wing, also the east wing) subtly combines dignified late-baroque façades with exuberant rococo interiors. Part of the ground floor is given over to the **Galerie der Romantik** (see page 67) at present, which boasts the Prussian monarchy's collection of 19th -century art. The ceremonial staircase which leads to Frederick the Great's state apartments has an abstract modern ceiling fresco by Hann Trier in place of the original decor which was destroyed by fire. Trier also painted the ceiling of the **Weiße Saal** (throne room and banquet hall).

The finest achievement of Knobelsdorff at Schloß Charlottenburg is the splendid 42-meter- (138-feet-) long **Goldene Galerie**. This rococo ballroom with its marble walls, dripping with gilded stucco, leads to two rooms containing a fine group of **Watteau paintings**. Frederick the Great was somewhat amused by the French artist's insolent *Enseigne du Gersaint*, a shop sign for art dealer Gersaint, in which a portrait of Louis XIV is being packed away rather unceremoniously. Among various other superb works by Watteau, you will find *L'amour paisible* (Quiet Love) and *Les Bergers* (The Shepherds).

Take a break for coffee or lunch at the **Orangerie**, or in the nearby Café Lenné (Spandauer Damm 3-5), then head off and explore the **Schloßpark**. Among the many buildings in the grounds, nearest to the palace is the Italian-style **Schinkel-Pavillon** (1825). As well as a collection of Schinkel's drawings and plans, the building contains early 19th-century Berlin paintings and porcelain. Upstairs, take a look at an amusing panorama of 1830s Berlin by Eduard Gaertner. North of the carp pond, the elegant **Belvedere**, once a teahouse, now houses a collection of quite exquisite 18th- and 19th-century porcelain.

West of Charlottenburg

Built for the Games of 1936, Hitler's **Olympiastadion** was spared bombardment to serve as headquarters for the British Army. The structure's bombastic gigantism is an eloquent testimony to the Führer's taste in architecture. Viewed from the main Olympic Gate, it appears to be very "low slung" until you see inside that the field itself has been sunk 12 meters (40 feet) below ground level. The 76,000-capacity stadium still stages sporting events, and from May through October is open daily to the public, except on event days.

The Porzellankabinett is filled with pieces of Chinese and Japanese porcelain.

To the west of the stadium, take the lift up the **Glockenturm** (bell tower) for a magnificent view over the Olympic site. Beyond the bell tower, a pathway will lead you to the **Waldbühne**, an open-air amphitheater which is a summer venue for concerts and films.

On Messedamm south east of the stadium, stands another colossus, the famous **ICC** (*International Congress Center*). One of the biggest convention centers in the world, the complex is also used for staging cultural events. Next to it on the equally huge **Messe und Ausstellungsgelände** (Trade Fair and Exhibition Area), the **Funk-**

turm (Radio Tower) is positively tiny—150 meters (492 feet) to the tip of its antenna, half the height of eastern Berlin's Television Tower (see page 50).

For breathtaking views, take the lift to the restaurant, 55 meters (180 feet) up, or the observation platform at the top. From here look south-west down the stretch of Autobahn called the **Avus** (*Automobil, Verkehrs, und Übungsstraße* — Vehicle, Traffic, and Training Road). Built in 1921, it was Germany's first racetrack. No longer used for racing, it now links Berlin city center to the westbound Autobahn.

Baroque and rococo decorations suffuse the Schloß Charlottenburg interior.

THE OUTSKIRTS

Northeast of Charlottenburg, the **Gedenkstätte Plötzensee** in Hüttigpfad is a stark and moving memorial to the victims of Nazi persecution (take bus 123 from S-Bahn Tiergarten to Plötzensee). On the opposite side of the road a lane leads past a modern juvenile correction center to the site of the prison where thousands of people were tortured and executed between 1933 and 1945, including many of the officers involved in the Stauffenberg plot (see page 38).

The dark sheds where executions were carried out have been preserved, and outside a stone urn, filled with soil from

Wannsee—where city-swellers come to let their hair down on warm days.

concentration camps, stands in a corner of the paved yard. In one of the sheds you will find a small and poignant exhibition of historical documents which includes death warrants and pictures of leading members of the German resistance. There is an information office opposite the main gate where you can obtain free booklets in English, Russian, and French.

About 35 km (22 miles) to the north of the city on the outskirts of the former East German town of Oranienburg, the site of another disturbing war memorial can be found.

The **Nationale Mahn- und Gedenkstätte Sachsenhausen** is a partially preserved Nazi concentration camp which was taken over by the Soviets after the war and used for internment. Horrifying statistics reveal that over 100,000 people were systematically executed here between 1936 and 1945. Some of the barrack blocks have been converted into museums and the former laundry now houses a chapel and cinema. Proposals to develop the former administrative buildings have been fiercely countered by those who believe they should be left in perpetuity. American architect Daniel Libeskind has contributed to the debate with proposals for selective flooding of the area and the construction of expressionistic memorial sculptures. It seems likely, however, that the monument will remain as it is for some years to come.

Grunewald and Wannsee

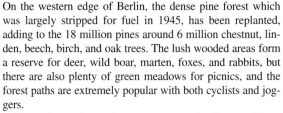

On the western edge of Berlin, the dense pine forest which was largely stripped for fuel in 1945, has been replanted, adding to the 18 million pines around 6 million chestnut, linden, beech, birch, and oak trees. The lush wooded areas form a reserve for deer, wild boar, marten, foxes, and rabbits, but there are also plenty of green meadows for picnics, and the forest paths are extremely popular with both cyclists and joggers.

The easiest and most direct way to get to the Grunewald is to take line S3 from Bahnhof Zoo to Grunewald S-Bahn station. Alternatively, you could combine your trip with a visit to the museums at Dahlem—the Brücke Museum is only a 20-minute walk from the eastern edge of the forest. Drivers take the Avus and turn off on the Hüttenweg to **Grunewaldsee**, a lake offering swimming and sandy beaches. On the east shore, in an attractive lakeside setting of beech trees, you will find the **Jagdschloß Grunewald**, a hunting lodge built in 1542 for Prince Elector Joachim II. Situated in a cobbled courtyard, the lodge has been restored to its original Renaissance appearance.

Inside is displayed a rather curious collection of early German hunting portraits and landscapes, among which can be found some remarkable paintings, in particular a series of panels depicting the Passion Cycle by Lucas Cranach. Other German and Dutch works of note are those by Jordaens, Rubens, and Bruyn.

There are marvellous views over the lake from the first- and second-floor rooms, and the period porcelain, furniture, and wooden floors add rustic charm. The nominal admission charge includes entry to the small hunting museum (*Waldmuseum*) on the opposite side of the courtyard. A short walk down the path outside the lodge brings you to the rather grand **Forsthaus Paulsborn**, where you can dine in splendour overlooking the lake.

On the Grunewald's west side, along Havelchaussee, the **Grunewaldturm** (Grunewald Tower) is a neo-Gothic tower built in 1897 to commemorate the 100th birthday of King Wilhelm I. You can climb the 205 steps to reach the 55-meter- (180-foot-) high observation platform for views as far as Potsdam. Ferry stations in the area offer boat rides on the River Havel and forest lakes, and the east bank of the Havel is lined with sandy beaches as far as the Wannsee lakes.

The waterfront near **Wannsee** S-Bahn station is a crowded spot where city-dwellers come and let their hair down on warm spring and summer days. The water bustles with pleasure boats and ferries, and you can cruise all the way to Spandau and Potsdam from here. **Strandbad Wannsee** is Berlin's biggest beach, and the longest inland one in Europe.

Teufelsberg—Devil's Mountain

At the beginning of the Grunewald, in the middle of the flat, northern European plain that stretches from Warsaw to the Netherlands, is a mountain. Aptly named Teufelsberg (Devil's Mountain), it is not tall—only 115 meters (380 feet)—but a mountain nevertheless, painstakingly created from a pile of rubble from World War II bombardments.

In summer, the hill is nicely grassed over for toddler mountain climbers to scramble on. In winter, snow creates an excellent toboggan run, a good nursery slope for skiers, and even two bone-rattling ski jumps. The flatness of the north European plain east of the mountain is demonstrated by the off-limits summit where military radar equipment operates as far as Asia.

West of the Großer Wannsee, Königstraße crosses Berliner Forst, an extension of the Grunewald to **Glienicke Park**. Its whimsical landscaping of little hills, bridges, and ponds was the work of Peter Josef Lenné in the early 19th century. **Schloß Glienicke** (1828) is a rather austere neo-classical edifice, but the nearby cloister, villa, and garden houses add a romantic touch.

A ferry links **Pfaueninsel** (Peacock Island), a delightfully tranquil nature reserve in the Havel, towards the northern edge of Berliner Forst. The island menagerie was used to stock Berlin Zoo, but the bird sanctuary still has much to offer the nature lover, including, of course, peacocks.

At the southern tip, half hidden in the trees, is Schinkel's Swiss Cottage, but the island's principal curiosity is the fake ruin **Schloß Pfaueninsel**, built in 1797 as a hideaway for Friedrich Wilhelm II and his lover, the Countess Wilhelmine von Lichtenau. The white wooden façade imitates granite blocks, and the delightful turrets are joined together at the top by a pretty bridge.

Königsstraße extends as far as an illustrious relic of the Cold War, **Glienicker Bridge**, once a restricted border crossing between West Berlin and East Germany where the KGB and CIA exchanged spies.

Spandau

With a history longer than Berlin's, **Spandau**, northwest of Berlin, still remains fiercely independent-minded, and was the most reluctant of the townships to be annexed by the metropolis in 1920. The town is easily reached by U-Bahn (line U7 to Rathaus Spandau) and, if you have time to spare, is well worth visiting for its old restored quarter and 16th-century citadel, the venue for regular summer festivals of jazz and classical music.

The **Altstadt** (old town) was less damaged by bombing than the rest of Berlin, and has been restored to much of its former charm. You will see pretty, gabled houses, Renaissance façades, and even traces of the 14th-century town wall along Hoher Steinweg, east of Falkenseer Platz.

Spandauers claim that **St. Nikolaikirche**, situated at the heart of Reformationsplatz, is where Prince Joachim II converted to Protestantism. The Gothic structure has an imposing Renaissance altar.

The 16th-century **Zitadelle** (citadel), in the River Havel, was the scene of heavy fighting in the Napoleonic Wars. Its walls enclose the old **Juliusturm**, a castle keep from prior medieval fortifications. It was the repository for gold coins paid by the French as reparations after the Franco-Prussian War, and returned as part payment for reparations following World War I. The **Heimatmuseum** (Local History Museum) in the Zitadelle contains an exhibition of Jewish gravestones, found during excavations here, which date back to the 13th century. A mock medieval tavern within offers good, solid fare in authentic surroundings.

If you're thinking of looking for it, *don't*—the famous **Spandau prison** was razed to the ground to make way for the building of a community center after the death in 1987 of its last (and latterly sole) inmate, convicted war-criminal Rudolf Hess.

To the north of the borough, **Spandauer Forst** is half the size of the Grunewald, but equally beautiful. The forest contains nature reserves where you will find rare plants protected in their wild state. **Teufelsbruch**, for example, which regularly records the coldest winter temperatures in Berlin, provides a natural shelter for shrubs and flowers from the sub-Arctic tundra. Just to the east of Teufelsbruch, summer bathing and camping are popular at **Bürgerablage** beach on the Havel.

Köpenick

With its delightful **Altstadt** (old town) of 18th- and 19th-century houses, the borough of Köpenick lies on the southern outskirts of eastern Berlin, and is easily accessible by S-Bahn line S3. The town is rapidly becoming a fashionable place to live, and many of its crumbling old houses are gradually being restored. Affluent shops are also starting to open their doors, not to mention restaurants, cafés, and art galleries.

Like Spandau in the west, Köpenick has a longer history than Berlin itself, having been a Slave settlement on an island in the Spree in the 9th century. It has a similarly independent-minded history. Socialist before the proclamation of the Weimar Republic, the town led the counter-assault which put an end to the right-wing Kapp Putsch of 1920 (see page 19). Resistance to Hitler by the town's workers in May 1933 resulted in the *Köpenicker Blutwoche* (bloodbath) in which storm-troopers killed 91 workers. A memorial to the event is in the former Prussian official jail at Puchanstraße 12.

To reach **Schloß Köpenick** take tram 86 along Bahnhofstraße to Schloßplatz. The attractive 17th-century palace occupies its own little island in the River Dahme, and is the occasional setting for open-air summer concerts.

Everything has its Price

Spandau suffered no more damage during World War II than it did at the hands of Napoleon's soldiers retreating from Russia in 1813. Prussian and Russian forces together laid siege to 3,000 French troops occupying Spandau Zitadelle. Berliners rode out to watch the fighting, keeping outside the range of the cannonade that was setting fire to scores of Spandau houses.

After the rout of the French, Berliners wanted to visit the citadel and take a peek at the burned-out houses. The canny people of Spandau charged admission and collected 4,335 thalers, which they used to rebuild their homes.

At Spandau Fortress it seems as if time has stood still.

The palace houses a **Kunstgewerbemuseum** (Arts and Crafts Museum), which is not quite as impressive as its counterpart in the Tiergarten (see page 71), but notable for a superb collection of Meissen porcelain, medieval gold jewellery, Venetian glass and 18th-century rococo furniture. Stop off at the museum café for a fine outlook over the river.

From Köpenick, a branch of the Spree leads to the **Großer Müggelsee**, the largest lake in Berlin, very pleasant for boat cruises or picnics on the shore.

MUSEUMS AND EXCURSIONS

After 1945, many works originally in the eastern half of the city or Potsdam were transferred to a new home in the west. Now, after reunification, Berlin's museums are again in a state of flux. With such changes the renovation of the Neues Museum (New Museum) on Museumsinsel, and the expansion of the Kulturforum in Tiergarten, some paintings and sculptures haved moved or may move. Since the relocation of collections seems to be a slow and ongoing process, check with the tourist office or a particular museum to make sure that a particular work is indeed on view.

Berlin has a huge number of museums, but luckily most of them are arranged in convenient groups. We have listed all the major museums in three sections, depending on their principal locations: Charlottenburg, Dahlem, Kreuzberg and the Tiergarten in western Berlin; Museumsinsel and Nikolaiviertel in eastern Berlin; and other important museums in eastern and western Berlin.

Museums are superbly laid out, and most provide leaflets (usually in German, but often in English and French) giving detailed information about the exhibits; you will find honesty boxes for payment freely dotted about. For opening hours, see pages 119–122. As a general rule, admission is free to many museums on public holidays and Sundays, too.

Charlottenburg

The museums in and around Schloß Charlottenburg are undergoing transformation, with the Greek and Roman antiquities recently joining the treasures of the Pergamonmuseum in eastern Berlin (see page 76) and other changes planned. The addresses given below apply for the foreseeable future.

Purchase a day pass (*Tageskarte*), which will admit you to the Classical Antiquities, Prehistory and Egyptian museums, as well as the Galerie der Romantik; a combination ticket (*Sammelkarte*) admits you to the palace itself (including a 1-hour guided tour of the royal apartments), the Belvedere, Golden Gallery and Schinkel Pavillon (see pages 55-56).

> Sign:
> *Eintritt frei-*
> admission free

Ägyptisches Museum – *Schloßstraße 70*
Housed in one of the two handsome, domed-roof guardhouses in front of the palace, the museum boasts one of the great-

est collections of Egyptian art to be found in Europe. It covers 3,000 years of sculpture, papyrus fragments, and hieroglyphic tablets.

The most famous piece is undoubtedly the beautiful head of **Queen Nefertiti** (1340 B.C.), consort of Akhenaton, which is displayed in a dramatically lit room on the second floor. The bust had been buried for more than 3,000 years before it was unearthed by German and French archaeologists in 1912. Downstairs, standing at the entrance to the former stables (**Marstall**), is the monumental **Kalabsha Gate** (20 B.C.), saved from the waters of the Aswan Dam in the 1960s. The stables constitute an impressive gallery, with a white arched ceiling supported by slender cast-iron columns.

Look out for the many other gems in the collection, in particular the wrinkled features of the **Berlin Green Head**, the restored **temple courtyard** of King Sahu-Re, a mummy and sarcophagi, and charming blue faience funerary objects in the form of animals.

Antikensammlung Charlottenburg
Sophie-Charlottestraße 17-18

This small museum contains some of Grek and Roman antiquities once housed in the Antikenmuseum, though the lion's share of the collections went to the Pergamonmuseum (see page 76).

Gift Hunting in Museums

Museum shops are a good place to find art posters, lithographs, and high-quality reproductions. In museums of classical antiquity such as the Ägyptisches Museum and the Pergamon, you can get excellent copies of Greek vases or ancient sculpture in bronze, plaster or resin. Museum shops also offer a certain guarantee of quality for genuine artisan products such as textiles, pottery, pewter, and woodcarving.

Galerie der Romantik
East Wing, Schloß Charlottenburg

The palace provides a fine setting for works by 19th-century Romantic painters, and boasts the most comprehensive collection of paintings by **Caspar David Friedrich** to be found in Germany. Among his works, look out for *Abtei im Eichwald* (Abbey in the Woods, 1809) and *Der Mönch am Meer* (The Monk by the Sea, 1810).

Note, too, Johann Hummel's curious study in perspective, a painting of the granite bowl which can still be seen in Berlin's Lustgarten, in front of the Altes Museum.

Haus der Zeitgenössischen Kunst – *Schloßstraße 1*

Occupying the former quarters of the Antikenmuseum, the House of Contemporary Art is based on the holdings of the Berggruen Sammlung Collection, with works by Picassoo and other, more recent, modernists.

Museum für Vor- und Frühgeschichte
West Wing, Schloß Charlottenburg

Berlin's museum of primeval and early history houses an extensive collection of artefacts from the Stone Age to the Bronze Age. The superbly presented exhibits and meticulously reconstructed dioramas are clearly described in English, French, and German.

Dahlem

The greatest concentration of Berlin's museums is currently in Dahlem, south west of Berlin. A large complex standing between Arnimallee and Lansstraße groups under one roof the Gemäldegalerie (Painting Gallery), the Skulpturengale-rie (Sculpture Gallery) and the museums of Ethnography and Far Eastern Art; as for the basement, it contains a junior museum and an exhibition for the blind. The Brücke Museum and Botanical Gardens, with its horticultural museum, are nearby.

To reach Dahlem, take the U-Bahn (line U2) from Witten-bergplatz to Dahlem-Dorf. Opposite the station, Café Zodia-co, Königin-Luise-Straße 44, is an excellent place to sit outside in summer for coffee or authentic Italian food.

Botanischer Garten und Museum
Königin-Luise-Straße 6-8

Tropical houses contain some 18,000 different species of ex-otic plants, and there's also a smell and touch garden for the blind. A small museum at the north entrance covers the his-tory and use of plants.

Brücke Museum – *Bussardsteig 9*

The Bridge Museum is an intimate, single-storey museum situated in a pleasant suburb about 20 minutes' walk from Jagdschloß Grunewald. Opposite Dahlem-Dorf U-Bahn sta-tion, take bus 180 to Clayallee, then bus 115 to Pückler-straße. The museum is 5 minutes from the bus stop.

The museum was created in 1967 to house works of clas-sical modernism, thanks to a legacy of Karl Schmidt-Rott-luff, a member of the Expressionist group *Die Brücke* which worked in Dresden from 1905 to 1913. A large number of the group's works were labelled as "degenerate" and thus destroyed by the Nazis. Schmidt-Rottluff's own bold paint-ings hang beside the works of fellow Expressionists Emil Nolde, Erich Heckel, Ernst Ludwig Kirchner, and Max Pechstein.

Gemäldegalerie – *Arnimallee 23-7*

This collection of European art from the 13th to the 18th cen-turies ranks among the most important in the world. Included here are paintings by Gainsborough, Botticelli, Raphael, Wat-teau, Canaletto, Holbein, Dürer, Cranach, Bruegel, Van Eyck and Rembrandt. By 1998 most of this collection will have been installed in the Neue Nationalgalerie in Tiergarten (see page 72). In the meantime, check with the museum and the

Some 18,000 different species of exotic plants are housed at the Botanischer Garten und Museum.

tourist office to determine if the masterpiece you wish to see is on view here or at the Neue Nationalgalerie.

Museen für Außereuropäische Kulturen
Lansstraße 8

The Museums of non-European cultures contain frescoes, murals, paintings, stone sculptures and delicate fabrics from India, Thailand, Tibet, Burma, Indonesia and Nepal, as well as Chinese, Japanese, and Korean art, including delicate paper hangings, wooden screens, paintings, carpets, ceramics and lacquerware.

Museum für Völkerkunde – *Lansstraße 8*

The Museum of Ethnology is a dazzling display of ethnic art and culture. Great for children.

Kreuzberg

Berlin Museum – *Lindenstraße 14*

The museum of municipal history, folklore and culture is opening again in 1998, after extensive renovations and the addition to the elegant baroque building of a controversial extension.

Designed by American architect Daniel Libeskind, the sharply angled design of the new extension is intended to represent the jagged course of German history; it will house the Jewish collection (currently split between the Berlin Museum and the Martin-Gropius-Bau, see below) as well as the museum's post-1800 works.

The museum has a fine collection of paintings of Berlin by Kirchner, Liebermann, Beckmann, and Corinth, and superb displays of porcelain. Authentically furnished rooms illustrate the life of the Berlin bourgeoisie from the more assertive age of neo-classical architect Karl Friedrich Schinkel, through the Biedermeier days of the mid-19th century to the lighter period of Jugendstil and the years leading up to the First World War. Upstairs a collection of toys, including an impressive dolls' house, dates from around the turn of the century, and women's clothes from the early 1800s to the 1970s are also featured.

Martin-Gropius-Bau – *Stresemannstraße 110*

The museum is the venue for major temporary exhibitions in Modernism, as well as the permanent home of the modern art collection of the Berlin gallery. Pending completion of the Berlin Museum extension (see above), a small (and rather disappointing) collection of memorabilia of the city's once flourishing Jewish community is presented in the **Jüdische Abteilung** (Jewish Department).

The **Berlinische Galerie** is located on the first floor and illustrates Berlin life from 1870 through to the present day in painting, sculpture, photography and architecture by the city's leading artists. In the attic, the **Werkbund-Archiv** is an impressive collection of 20th-century arts and crafts.

Deutsches Technikmuseum Berlin

Trebbiner Straße 9

A mural on the wall facing the Landwehr canal gives you an idea of the treats in store in Berlin's Technology Museum.

Erected over the railway goods yards of the old Anhalter Bahnhof (see p.41), the museum is devoted not only to rail traffic, but also to aircraft, shipping and automobiles, plus the technology of textiles, medicine, communications and printing. Visitors are encouraged to manipulate various machines and participate in scientific experiments.

Tiergarten

Bauhaus-Archiv Museum für Gestaltung
Klingelhöferstraße 13-14

The museum documents the achievements of the most progressive 20th-century European school of architecture and design. Architects Walter Gropius, Mies Van der Rohe, and Marcel Breuer, along with artists Paul Klee, Vasili Kandinsky, Lyonel Feininger Oskar Schlemmer, and Laszlo Moholy-Nagy attempted to integrate arts, crafts, and architecture into mass industrial society. On view here is a selection of the objects they created: tubular steel chairs, cups and saucers, teapots, desks, new weaves for carpets, chess pieces, and children's building blocks, as well as some pioneering architectural plans and sketches.

There's a reference library upstairs, and a small café offers refreshments.

Hamburger Bahnhof Museum für Gegenwart
Invalidenstraße 50

A former train station is the stunning setting for works by Erich Marx, Andy Warhol, Anselm Kiefer, and other 20th-century artists.

Kunstgewerbemuseum – Matthäikirchplatz

Outstanding in the Arts and Crafts Museum's dazzling collection of jewellery is the **Welfenschatz** (Guelphs' treasure). These splendid examples of the goldsmith's art from the 11th to 15th centuries—richly bejewelled crosses, reliquaries, and portable altars—were presented to St. Blasius Cathedral in Brunswick by succeeding generations of Guelph dukes. Other prized exhibits include glazed Italian majolica and a quite bewitching collection of porcelain— Chinese, Meissen, Frankenthaler, Nymphenburger as well as the city's own Königliche Porzellan Manufaktur (the royal KPM).

Kupferstichkabinett – *Matthäikirchplatz*
The drawings and prints to be found in the reunited Engravings Collection were recently transferred from the Altes Museum and Gemäldegalerie and range from 14th-century illuminated manuscripts to modern woodcuts by Erich Heckel and lithographs by Willem de Kooning. Also on display are outstanding works by Dürer, Botticelli, and Rembrandt.

Musikinstrumentenmuseum – *Tiergartenstraße 1*
Amongst the museum's many historical musical instruments are a 1703 Stradivarius violin, the 1810 piano of composer Carl Maria von Weber, and a 1929 New York Wurlitzer cinema organ, which comes alive in a concert given at noon the first Saturday of every month. Tours are conducted every Saturday at 11am.

Neue Nationalgalerie – *Potsdamer Straße 50*
The gallery houses permanent collections of 19th- and 20th-century painting and sculpture, and is the venue for many excellent temporary exhibitions of contemporary art. As of 1998, a new wing houses an impressive collection of art from the 14th through 18th centuries – including many works from the Gemäldegalerie in Dahlem, among them such masterpieces as Hans Holbein's portrait of Georg Gisze (1532); the rather amusing *The Fountain of Youth* (1546) by Lucas Cranach the Elder; Van Eyck's *Portrait of Giovanni Arnolfini* (1440); Van Dyck's portraits of a Genoese couple (1626); Vermeer's study, *Young Lady with a*

Pearl Necklace (1664), and among one of the largest Rembrandt collections in the world, a portrait of the artist's second wife, Hendrickje Stoffels (1659). After the Nazi confiscation of "Degenerate Art," the gallery is gradually piecing together its modern collection. Look out for paintings by Van Gogh, Monet, Corot, Pissarro, Manet, Renoir, Cézanne, Degas, Rousseau, Beckmann, Dix, Klee, Munch, Grosz, Gauguin, Magritte, Picasso and Dali. American artists in the permanent collection include Mark Rothko. Sculpture includes works by Rodin.

Museumsinsel

The main cluster of museums in eastern Berlin stands on an island in the River Spree. Buy a *Tageskarte* which will admit you to the Pergamon and Bode Museums, the Nationalgalerie, Otto-Nagel-Haus, as well as the Schinkel Museum in the Friedrichwerderschen Kirche.

Alte Nationalgalerie – *Bodestraße 1*

Although its collection was depleted both by Hitler's assault on *Entartete Kunst* (degenerate art) and the ravages of war,

"Form follows function" is the guiding principle behind the works at Bauhaus Archiv.

the museum, which is undergoing extensive renovations, has some interesting **German works** of the 19th and 20th centuries: Blechen, Waldmüller, Slevogt, Liebermann (*The Flax Workers* and portraits of Wilhelm von Bode and Richard Strauss). Von Menzel's *Eisenwalzwerk* (The Iron Foundry, 1875) is a striking portrayal of industrial labour, and Oskar Kokoschka's painting, *Pariser Platz* (1926), recalls the bustle around the Brandenburg Gate during the twenties. The *Brücke* school of Expressionists has works by Nolde, Heckel, Schmidt-Rottluff, and Kirchner. Later Expressionists include Otto Dix, Grosz, and Corinth.

The small collection of European painting has works by Goya, Courbet, Degas, and Cézanne, while sculpture is represented in works by Rodin and Käthe Kollwitz. While 20th-century works are slowly being moved to the Neue Nationalgalerie and other Berlin museums, the Alte Nationalgalerie is becoming the city's major repository for 19th-century art.

Altes Museum – Lustgarten

The first of the museums on Museumsinsel. Notice in front the polished granite bowl which was originally intended to sit atop the edifice. At present the museum houses 19th-century works by Renoir, Manet, and Van Gogh, as well as temporary exhibitions.

Bodemuseum – Entrance on Monbijoubrücke

The museum groups Egyptian, Early Christian, Byzantine and European art in a neo-baroque interior.

The museum's collections have expanded recently with the magnificent romanesque, Gothic, and Renaissance sculptures that were formerly housed in the Skulpturengalerie in Dahlem. In the **Egyptian collection** is the unfinished sandstone head of a queen (14th century B.C.). The subject is probably Nefertiti, bringing a complement of grace and serenity to the beauty of the painted head on display in the Charlottenburg Museum (see page 65).

In the **Early Christian and Byzantine** department, look out for a 6th-century **Ravenna mosaic** from the church of San Michele, depicting Jesus as a young teacher and later, bearded, at the Day of Judgment.

As American troops retrieved the Berlin art treasures stored in Thuringia, most of the best ended up in Dahlem rather than on the Museuminsel. But the Bode's **European paintings** do include

Located on the banks of the Spree, the Bode has an impressive collection of European masterworks.

The present stands in awe of the past — ancient Processional Street at the Pergamonmuseum.

works by Cranach, Elsheimer, Van Ruisdael, Bloemaert and Poussin.

Pergamonmuseum –
Kupfergraben

The home of many magnificent works of classical antiquity, the Near East, Islam and the Orient, the museum is named after its most prized possession: the gigantic **Pergamon Altar** (2nd century B.C.). This masterpiece of Hellenistic art comes from what is now Bergama, near the west coast of Turkey. The massive colonnaded altar, which is dedicated to Zeus and Athena, has been constructed to fill one hall of the museum.

The **Babylonian Processional Street** (604-562 B.C.), built by King Nebuchadnezzar II, is equally impressive. Lions sculpted in relief stride along the street's blue and ochre tiled walls towards the Ishtar Gate. The gate itself is decorated with bulls and dragons, also in blue and ochre tile.

A third great treasure is the Roman **Market gate of Miletus**, from Greek Asia Minor (A.D. 165). Its name belies the true character of this elaborately pedimented monument, which constitutes both gateway and shopping complex.

The **Islamic Museum**, in the Pergamon's south wing exhibits the grand façade of the 8th-century **Palace of Mshatta** (from modern Jordan). It is embellished with intricately incised or perforated animal or plant motifs. In fact, a German art historian rescued this *tour de force* of early Islamic decoration at the turn of the century by persuading the Sultan of Turkey not to use it as building material for a railway link to Mecca. The Islamic collection has recently been enhanced with the addition of carpets, wood screens, and ceramics. Among the other precious exhibits you will find some exquisite Indian **Mogul miniatures**.

Nikolaiviertel

This neighbourhood has been reconstructed and preserved as an extension of the Märkisches Museum, and presents a composite picture of life in the city from the Middle Ages to the 19th century.

Märkisches Museum – *Am Köllnischen Park 5*
Situated near Inselbrücke on the south bank of the River Spree, the museum has a curious collection of Berliniana: the first sewing machines, bicycles, telephones, an 1881 telephone book with 41 names, a 19th-century worker's kitchen, and a model of the infamous tenements that nurtured unrest prior to the 1848 revolution.

Nikolaikirche – *Nikolaikirchplatz*
Berlin's oldest church contains an interesting collection which chronicles the history of the Berlin and Cölln townships from the 13th through 17th centuries, including Gothic, Renaissance, and baroque church sculpture.

Otto-Nagel-Haus – *Märkisches Ufer 16-18*
This is a small museum devoted to radical artists and photographers from the November Revolution to the present day.

Schinkel-Museum
Werdersche Markt, in the Friedrichswerdersche Kirche
Statues by Schinkel as well as Schadow and others are displayed in the hushed setting of the brick church designed by the architect.

Other Important Museums

Brecht-Weigel-Haus – *Chausseestraße 125*
The house where playwright Bertolt Brecht spent the last three years of his life has been preserved as a small museum, and the rooms are filled with memorabilia. The playwright is buried in the Dorotheenstädtische cemetery nearby.

Bröhan-Museum – *Schloßstraße 1a*
Situated near Schloß Charlottenburg, this museum contains beautiful Art-Deco and Art-Nouveau paintings, porcelain, furniture, and silver.

Käthe-Kollwitz Museum – *Fasanenstraße 24*
An intimate museum containing sketches and sculptures by Berlin artist Käthe Kollwitz, is housed in an elegant villa near the Ku'damm. Tape tours are available in English.

Potsdam

If you have time to spare, a visit to the elegant old baroque town of Potsdam is an absolute must. Stroll round the summer palaces of Frederick the Great and other Prussian monarchs, or wander amongst the attractively restored 18th-century architecture in the center of town.

Potsdam is situated around 30 km (19 miles) southwest of Berlin. The most direct route is by S-Bahn (Line S3) from Bahnhof Zoo to Potsdam Stadt; alternatively, you can get off at Wannsee and take the bus or boat.

Park Sanssouci

Potsdam's main attractions are the summer palaces and
gardens at Sanssouci, built in the 18th and 19th centuries.
The grounds are filled with charming palaces, pavilions,
fountains, and temples. (Note that many of the buildings
are currently being renovated, so check with the tourist information office to find out if opening times are affected.)

Schloß Sanssouci, was commissioned by Frederick the
Great and designed by Knobelsdorff in 1744 from the
king's own sketches. For the most stunning approach, follow the Allee nach Sanssouci from Luisenplatz leading up
to the palace. Make your way to the other side of the
palace where you will find a large courtyard surrounded
by semicircular colonnades. The rooms inside the palace
can be visited only by guided tour (in German), and are
very popular.

The tour includes Frederick's splendid **Konzertsaal** (Concert Chamber) where walls and ceiling are overlaid with a
delicate gilt filigree. At the center of the palace, the **Marmor-
saal** (Marble Hall) contains exquisite columns made from
Carrara marble and stucco figures perched high up on the cor-
nice. Among the guest rooms to be visited, the yellow
Voltaire room boasts bizarre rococo decorations including
wooden parrots hanging from perches.

The royal **Bildergalerie** (Picture Gallery) was designed to
house Frederick the Great's extensive collection of paintings
by masters such as Caravaggio, and Rubens.

A path through the woods southwest of the palace leads to
the **Chinesisches Teehaus**. On top sits a gilded mandarin
under a sunshade, while more statues surround the base. Inside, you'll find a fine collection of Chinese porcelain.

A stroll west along Hauptweg brings you to a vast structure built from red brick and white sandstone, which is cov-

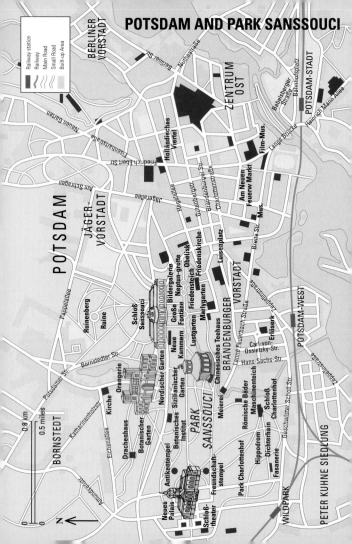

POTSDAM AND PARK SANSSOUCI

ered in rococo statuary. The **Neues Palais** (New Palace) is the largest of all the buildings in Park Sanssouci. The apartments can only be visited by guided tour (in German) which lasts about an hour.

Other highlights to be seen include the **Römische Bäder** (Roman Baths), by Schinkel, and **Schloß Charlottenhof**. To the north is the vast Italian Renaissance-style **Orangerie**, while the **Drachenhaus** (Dragon House), northwest of the park, serves refreshments.

Beside the lake, north of the town center is **Neuer Garten,** a pleasant English-style garden. It provides the perfect setting for **Schloß Cecilienhof** (1916), the ivy-covered, half-timbered pastiche of an English country manor built for Crown Prince Wilhelm and his wife. Winston Churchill, Joseph Stalin and Harry Truman met here in July 1945 to draw up the Potsdam Agreement that fixed the division of Germany for the next 45 years.

Babelsberg

The small suburb of **Babelsberg**, to the east of Potsdam, was home to the film industry which rivalled Hollywood in the 1920s. Classics such as Fritz Lang's *Metropolis* were made here. Now run as a studio and adventure park, **DEFA-Studio Babelsberg** organizes guided tours. Also here you will find vintage cars and stunt shows.

On the outskirts of Babelsberg, Albert-Einsteinstraße climbs Telegrafenberg to the bizarre **Einsteinturm**, built in 1921 as an astrophysics observatory. Albert Einstein was present here at a memorable technical demonstration of his Theory of Relativity. For want of a fitting statue to the great man, observatory staff have placed in the entrance hall, as a splendidly atrocious visual pun, a simple small stone—*Ein Stein*.

WHAT TO DO

In this liveliest of all German cities, there is no lack of activities once your sightseeing day is done. Whatever the vagaries of world politics, Berlin has never relinquished its role as national capital in the realm of the arts or shopping.

ENTERTAINMENT

Berliners are the most assiduous concert- and theater-goers in Europe, and you have to plan ahead if you want good tickets for the main events. Ask your travel agency or the German national tourist office for details of upcoming programmes, and book in advance where possible. The newspaper *Die Zeit*, published weekly and on sale outside Germany, has programmes of plays, concerts, and art exhibitions. In addition to the monthly publication *Berlin Programm*, produced by the tourist office, there are two fortnightly listings magazines, *Tip* and *Zitty*, which give full details and reviews. *Checkpoint*, an excellent monthly magazine in English, mixes features, tourist information, and listings, as *Berlin, Das Magazin*, a quarterly magazine published in German and English.

> **Don't be surprised to find out that a glass of beer is often cheaper than a coke.**

Music

Symphonic music in Berlin is fueled by three of the world's greatest orchestras. The Berliner Philharmoniker, housed in the Philharmonie (see page 39) achieved glory under the late Herbert von Karajan The highly rated Radio Symphony Orchestra Berlin also performs there, and concerts by the Berlin Symphony Orchestra can be heard in the Apollo-Saal of the Deutsche Staatsoper on Unter den Linden, and in Schinkel's beautifully restored Schauspielhaus on Gendarmenmarkt.

There's something to satisfy every musical taste in Berlin, from opera to live jazz sessions.

Chamber music and *Lieder* (song) recitals take place in the Kammermusiksaal(at the rear of the Philharmonie), in the Ephraimpalais (Nikolaiviertel), the Akademie der Künste (Hansaviertel) and the Hochschule der Künste, Hardenbergstraße 33.

Berlin's **Opera** lovers are well served by the Deutsche Oper in Bismarckstraße, the Deutsche Staatsoper on Unter den Linden, and the Komische Oper in Behrenstraße.

Jazz and **rock** concerts are usually performed in big halls such as the Deutschlandhalle, Philharmonie, Neuer Friedrichstadtpalast and Olympiastadion or in dozens of cafés and small *Musikkneipen* (music bars).

Theatre

When it comes to theater, Berlin is one of the most exciting and innovative cities in Europe and the world, so that even without a great command of the German language, any enthusiastic theatregoer can enjoy some stirring performances.

In Germany major theaters often maintain several productions in repertory, so that in any one week you will be able to see the same troupe perform contemporary or classical drama.

Since reunification, the city has found that it has more theaters than it can cope with, and several establishments are facing closure. Check with the tourist information office. The theatres we list below look set to remain open.

The city's most audacious and versatile repertory is based at the **Schaubühne** (Ku'damm and Lehninerplatz). Its almost brutally uncompromising performances of classical avant-garde and experimental theater have achieved international renown. The stance is perpetually provocative, delighting in wrong-footing German society and questioning the blessings of German unification, as well as pointing out the dubious virtues of capitalist freedoms.

The city's **Fringe theatre** groups (*freie Gruppen*) come and quickly go, rather like brilliant shooting stars. In order to set themselves apart from the meretricious commercial theater, they often sport names such as Atelier International Kunst (Dahlmannstraße 11) or Theatermanufaktur (based at Hallesches Ufer 32).

Commercial theatre is not to be sneezed at, either. For the equivalents of Broadway or Shaftesbury Avenue musicals, operettas and comedies, try the very professional Theater am Kurfürstendamm (Kurfürstendamm 209), the Komödie (Kurfürstendamm 206), and the popular Theater des Westens (Kantstraße 12).

Eastern Berlin has also contributed to the ongoing theatre tradition, thanks largely to the efforts of its best-known playwright, Bertolt Brecht, who founded the world-renowned **Berliner Ensemble** (Bertolt-Brecht-Platz 1). Unsurprisingly, Brecht's own plays dominate the repertory, although it does expand to other, mostly modern, classics. **Contemporary plays** are staged at the Maxim-Gorki-Theater (Am Festungs-graben 2), and the **classics** at the Deutsches Theater (Schumannstraße 13a), the former home of theatre producer Max Reinhardt. At the Metropol-Theater (Friedrichstraße 101–102) you can enjoy rather lighter entertainment.

Other entertainment

Another long-standing Berlin tradition, at its heyday in the 1920s, **satirical cabaret** has always, by its very nature, had to struggle for its existence. Berlin has seemed to provide the necessary raw material, a perennially turbulent history to which reunification has not put a stop. Three survivors among the countless fly-by-nights are *Die Stachelschweine* (The Porcupines, Europa-Center), *Die Wühlmäuse* (The Voles, Nürnberger Straße 33) and *Die Distel* (The Thistle, Friedrichstraße 101). However, unless your German is excellent and you have an in-depth understanding of the political scene, this kind of cabaret will be almost impossible to follow.

Nightclubs range from garish girlie shows to conventional discos. In between are the transvestite shows, which can be saucy, often witty, occasionally outrageous but only rarely offensive. They offer an amusing perspective of Berlin's past with their impersonations of the great Marlene Dietrich and other such inimitables.

As befits a city which every February hosts a major International Film Festival, Berlin is endowed with a huge number of **cinemas**, showing a variety of films ranging from the usual Hollywood blockbusters to avant-garde works of art.

Most foreign-language films are usually dubbed into German, though some cinemas will occasionally show films in the original version. The letters to look out for are "OF" (*Originalfassung* — original version).

> Nowadays, many people regard the word *Fräulein* old-fashioned and improper.

Gamblers who don't require a glamorous Monte Carlo setting will find roulette, blackjack, and baccarat at the very modern **casino** (*Spielbank*) in the Europa-Center, as well as in some of the big hotels in eastern Berlin.

SPORTS

Thanks to its many lakes and rivers, Berlin does not lack opportunities for **swimming**, and has around 20 beaches, most of them pleasantly sandy. Continuing the old Prussian devotion to physical culture, a few of the beaches are reserved for nude bathing — or FKK, as you may see it signposted. The most popular of these beaches are the Bullenwinkel on the Grunewaldsee and Strandbad Halensee on the Teufelssee. If you would rather wear a swimsuit, try the lovely beaches of the Wannsee, Glienicker See, the Havel, or the less crowded Großer Müggelsee in eastern Berlin, and Templiner See, out at Potsdam.

Throughout the city you will find numerous open-air and indoor **swimming pools**. Berlin's Luft und Badeparadies, *Blub* for short, at Buschkrugallee 64, Neukölln, is a huge water recreation center, offering both indoor and outdoor facilities, wave and surf pools, water slides, a solarium, sauna, and restaurants.

At Berlin's lakes, you will be able to rent equipment for many different types of **watersports**, including waterskiing, canoeing, rowing, sailing, and windsurfing.

If you fancy a spot of **fishing**, get yourself a good barbecued supper of white fish, pike perch or eel from the Havel, Müggelsee, and the Glienicker See. The Berlin tourist information center (see page 126) will give you details about licences and boat hire.

The Grunewald has the best trails for **horseback riding**. Hire a mount at Onkel Toms Hütte, Zehlendorf. Ponies are available for children to ride in Wittenau and Marienfelde.

Golf enthusiasts can get a round in at the Wannsee Club, Stölpchenweg. Your membership from your home club should gain you entrance.

With the huge successes of Boris Becker, Steffi Graf, and Michael Stich, **tennis** has now become a favourite

Making a splash — Wannsee is the perfect summer venue for watersports of all kinds.

national sport, with **squash** catching on fast, too. Both are well served, so to speak, at courts citywide, notably Paulsborner Straße (a few steps from the Ku'damm) and Brandenburgische Straße.

One surprise sport you may not have expected to practise in Berlin is **hang-gliding**, but it is in fact possible to throw yourself off the Teufelsberg, where you can also do a little **skiing** and **sledding** in winter (see page 60).

Try **roller skating** in summer or **ice-skating** in winter at the rink in Wilmersdorf (Fritz-Wildungs-Straße 9). The most pleasant defence against the aggressiveness of the city's **bicycle** riders is to rent one yourself at the Fahrradbüro Berlin, Hauptstraße 146. In the Tiergarten, meanwhile, **joggers** and roller skaters maintain a relationship of mutual disrespect.

Spectator Sports

You can go and watch the local professional **football** teams at the Olympic Stadium and the Friedrich-Ludwig-Jahn-Sportpark. **Ice hockey** can be seen at the Eissporthalle and international **rowing** regattas on the Hohenzollern canal. International **tennis** tournaments are held at the Rot-Weiß club. **Horse-racing** enthusiasts can watch trotting (*Trabrennen*) at Karlshorst (Treskowallee 129) or Mariendorf (Mariendorfer Damm 222). Last, but by no means least, the **Berlin Marathon** can be enjoyed from the sidelines throughout the city every autumn. The finishing line is situated at the Kaiser Wilhelm Memorial Church on Breitschiedplatz.

SHOPPING

Where to Shop

One thing reunification hasn't managed to change overnight is the division between poor east and consumer west. Although some smart shops have begun to emerge in eastrn Brlin, most notably along Friedrichstraße, where huge shopping complexes are going up, it will be some time before the east poses a threat to the luxury boutiques on and around Ku'damm.

The easy exchange of goods through the EIL and the Germans' taste for things foreign mean that you can find almost anything here from almost anywhere in the world. However, the Germans' high standard of living also means a high price tag on most imported goods, so you are better off buying "Made in Germany."

Trendy boutiques and large department stores like **Wertheim** line the Ku'damm itself, while the cherished institution of **KaDeWe** on Wittenbergplatz, and the **Europa-Center**, a multistorey shopping mall, are close at hand. **Shopping arcades** like Ku'damm-Karree (on the corner of Uhlandstraße), Ku'damm-Eck (in front of Café Kranzler), and the Fasanen-Uhland-Passage (off Fasanenstraße) are also worth a look. Many elegant shopping streets lead off to the north and south of the Ku'damm.

Most of the city's shops are open from 9:00 A.M. until 8:00 P.M. Monday – Friday. But many shops, especially in quiet neighborhoods, may close earlier. On Saturdays most shops are open from 9:00 A.M. until 4:00 P.M. Except for those in major trainstations and airports, shops are closed on Sundays.

What to Buy

Antiques

Pause a while from shopping in front of the Europa-Center's intriguing thermal clock.

Any moderately priced furniture or porcelain that claims to be Baroque or Rococo is probably a copy. Your best bet is to concentrate on products of the 19th sand early 20th centuries. Try looking down some of the side-streets off the Ku'damm.

Books

For book lovers, the bookshops on and around Savignyplatz offer a superb selection of books on art and design, architecture, fashion, and film. The capital is home to many secondhand and antiquarian bookshops, especially on Schlüterstraße and Knesebeckstraße. For books in English, the British

Bookshop at Mauerstraße 83–84, has a good range. Andenbuch in Knesebeckstraße has books in French, Spanish, and Italian.

Bric-a-brac

Collectors of faded old photos, period clothes, and other souvenirs from the past will love rummaging around in Berlin's many flea markets. Among the best are the Berliner Antik- und Flohmarkt located in the S-Bahn arches beneath Bahnhof Friedrichstraße (closed on Tuesday), and the Zillehof in Fasanenstraße (open Monday to Saturday). A huge selection of second-hand records, *objets d'art,* and clothes can be found at the weekend flea market on the Straße des 17. Juni in Charlottenburg, while Cold War memorabilia is on sale in front of the Brandenburg Gate. A word of caution: any "guaranteed genuine" bits of Wall are guaranteed only to be genuine fakes.

Make for the Turkish Market (*Türkischer Wochenmarkt*) on the Landwehr canal's Maybachufer in Kreuzberg to buy exotic food, spices, and utensils. (Open Tuesday and Friday afternoons.)

Berlin's colourful open-air markets are just the place for souvenir-hunting.

Calendar of Events

For the most up-to-date information on the city's festivals and arts calendar, consult the tourist office, the monthly Berlin Programm, or the local press. The following list gives a flavour of some of the major events.

January: *Berliner Musiktage*. A three-week contemporary music festival.

February: *Internationale Filmfestspiele Berlin*. Berlin's International Film Festival, in late February, rivals Cannes and Venice.

March/April: *Freie Berliner Kunstausstellung* (FBK). Exhibitions of art by major Berlin painters; *Klassische Musikfesttage* (classical music festival): Staatsoper Unter den Linden.

May: *Theatertreffen*. A German-language theatre festival with productions from all over Germany, Austria, and Switzerland.

June: Gay and Lesbian Festical. Largest event of its kind in Europe. Markets, food, performances.

July/August: Open-air classical music concerts by the Berlin Philharmonic at the Waldbühne; *Berliner Bachtage* (Bach Days Berlin) celebrates the music of Bach and other Baroque composers; Love Parade includes colourful parade, Rave, and Techno-music concerts at night.

September/October: Berlin Marathon; *Berliner Festwochen*, a major international festival of opera, theater, dance, music, and art.

October/November: *JazzFest Berlin*. A festival featuring both mainstream and avant-garde jazz.

December: *Weihnachtsmarkt*. Traditional Christmas markets are held on Breitscheidplatz and throughout the city.

Gourmet Delicacies

If you want to take back an edible souvenir, make sure you know your country's regulations governing the import of certain types of food. Among the pastries and cakes which travel best are *Lebkuchen* (gingerbread), *Spekulatius* (spiced Christmas cookies) and marzipan. KaDeWe's *Feinschmeckere-tage* offers 500 different breads, and 1,500 different types of cheese plus rare eastern delicacies, exotic teas, hand-made chocolates, and Beluga caviar. Berlin has no local wine, but plenty of wine shops to satisfy all connoisseurs of the best Rhine, Mosel, and Baden Württemberg vintages.

Music, Videos, and Cameras

The land of Bach and Beethoven offers a range of CDs, records, and tapes second only to that of the US. One of the best places to go is FNAC at Meinekestraße 23, which also stocks videos and photo equipment. Make sure any video tapes you purchase are compatible with your equipment at home.

Porcelain and Linen

Look out for modern Rosenthal and the local Königliche Porzellan Manufaktur (KPM), which was launched by Frederick the Great in the 18th century. The KPM shop on the factory premises at Wegely Straße 1 sells reduced price seconds, and there is also a shop at Kurfürstendamm 26a. Other celebrated manufacturers represented in Berlin, particularly in the antique shops, are Meissen, Nymphenburg of Munich, and Frankenthal.

Bed- and table-linens are of the finest quality. The duck- or goose-down *Federbett* (duvet) is a lifetime investment. Apart from the warm-as-toast winter model, look out for the lightweight one, for summer.

EATING OUT

Berlin has a great variety of cuisine than any other German city, offering anything from Japanese, Hungarian, Italian, and Czech to Arabic, Turkish, and Indonesian. A new German cuisine (*neue deutsche Küche*) has also emerged in response to a demand for greater culinary refinement. It doesn't mean that good old German dishes are being replaced by French imitations, but more and more they are being prepared with a new delicacy and imagination.

When to Eat

Mealtimes are quite flexible in Berlin, and you can always find something to eat somewhere at virtually any time of day or night. Breakfast (*Frühstück*) is the most important meal of the day, and generally consists of a selection of rolls, boiled eggs, cheese, muesli and honey, cold meats, fruit juices and either coffee or tea. In hotels it can be served from as early as 6am until 11am, while many cafés offer a selection of breakfasts from about 9 or 10 AM until as late as 6 PM.

A popular tradition in many eating places is the morning buffet, *Frühstücksbuffet*, where you help yourself from the counter to as much as you can eat for a fixed price. Berliners take lunch (*Mittagessen*) less seriously than other Germans, probably because the presence of so many fast-food (*Imbiß*) joints leads to constant snacking. In the evening, restaurants tend to fill up early and you should book in advance for the better establishments.

Where to Eat

Choices range from high-class *Restaurant* and bourgeois *Gaststätte* via the rather chic and arty *Bistro* or *Café* down to the popular *Kneipe*, originally student slang for any corner bar or tavern where you can have a drink and a snack big enough to call a meal. All of these places spill out onto the streets and squares as soon as the weather is warm enough, most notably on the Ku'damm and around Savignyplatz.

The *Konditorei* (café-cum-pastry shop) is in a separate category all of its own. In this bourgeois paradise, and armed with a newspaper attached to a rod, you can indulge in the great German tradition of *Kaffee und Kuchen*, enjoyed by all.

As well as cakes and pastries, ice-cream, coffee, tea, hot chocolate, fruit juices,and even wines, most places also offer a few light snacks and salads to stave off the hunger pangs. Undoubtedly, two of the most popular are Café Kranzler and Café Möhring, both on the Ku'damm, though the opulent Operncafé on Unter den Linden is a worthy rival, with a huge daily selection of exquisite home-made cakes.

For sheer decadence, indulge in the *Feinschmeckeretage*, the deli department on the sixth floor of KaDeWe, where you can enjoy a quite dazzling array of delicious foods from all around the world.

Cafés provide an excellent place just to sit and watch the world rush by while you relax. It's possible just to order a cup of coffee and then sit for hours without feeling pressured to leave, but you can also dine extremely well in Berlin cafés for little expense.

> If a table is occupied but has some chairs, just ask whether a seat is still available: *Ist hier noch frei?* (eest here nock frye?)

Whether *Brauhaus* (literally brewery) or *Bierkeller*, the old beer-halls continue to thrive, and become *Biergarten* in the parks. Two popular beer gardens in Dahlem serving hearty German fare are the Luise at Königin-Luise-Straße 40, and the Alter Krug at Königin-Luise-Straße 52. (Go to pages 137 – 144 for a list of recommended restaurants.)

Any Berliner will tell you that Café Kranzler is the place to see — and be seen in.

A menu (*Speisekarte*) is displayed outside most restaurants. Besides the à la carte menu, there are usually one or more set menus (*Menü* or *Gedeck*). The service charge (*Bedienung*) and value-added tax (*Mwst*) are usually included.

What to Eat

Soups and Starters

Appetizers (or starters) can be found listed on the menu under *Vorspeisen, Kleine Gerichte,* or *Kalte Platten.* Soups (*Suppen*) and stews (*Eintopfgerichte*) are often very hearty; sometimes, they can be enough for a whole meal. In Berlin, you can sample all the traditional German soups. The *Leberknödelsuppe* comes with spicy dumplings of flour, breadcrumbs, ox liver, onions, marjoram, and garlic. Served at its best, *Kartoffelsuppe* is a rich combination of potato, leeks, parsnips, celery, and bacon, while *Bohnensuppe* is a hearty concoction of several varieties of beans. The city's favourite, however, is plain old lentil soup (*Linsensuppe*), best with pieces of sausage in it.

The following two are typical starters: *Hackepeter*, the German version of steak tartare, and *Soleier*, eggs pickled in brine (*Sole*), then peeled and halved and seasoned with salt, pepper, paprika, vinegar, and oil. They are generally eaten with the ubiquitous Berlin mustard — *Mostrich*.

Main Dishes

Fish is served fresh from the River Havel. Try specialities like *Havelaal grün*, eel boiled in a dill sauce, or *Havelzander*, pike-perch served with *Salzkartoffeln*, simple (but surprisingly tasty) boiled potatoes. This very humble vegetable is something of a Berlin obsession. One of the city's great gourmet delights is the *Kartoffelpuffer*, a sort of potato pancake; *Kartoffelsalat* (potato salad) is also popular.

The supreme Berlin delicacy is undoubtedly *Eisbein mit Sauerkraut und Erbsenpüree* — pig's knuckle on a purée of peas with sauerkraut prepared in white wine, juniper berries, caraway seeds, and cloves. And a generous dollop of mustard, as always. A little more humble, but just as fine, is *gebratene Leber*, also known as *Leber Berliner Art*, sautéed liver served with slices of apple and browned onion rings.

The original recipe for *Kasseler Rippen*, or smoked pork chops, came not from the town of Kassel, but from a Berlin butcher by the name of Kassel. Berlin also claims as its own two world-famous sausages: the giant *Bockwurst* (a type of boiled sausage), so named because a local butcher advertised it suspended between the mouths of two goats (*Bock*); and the Viennese sausage, or *Wiener*, was invented, so they say, in Berlin.

In this predominantly meat-oriented culture, vegetarians may end up feeling rather excluded. The good news, however, is that a number of places are beginning to include vegetarian dishes on their menus. *Gemüsestrudel*, (a type of vegetable strudel) is made from courgettes, onions, sweetcorn, peppers, and broccoli in a spicy tomato sauce, and wrapped in flaky pastry. *Ofenkartoffel mit Kräuterquark* (baked potato filled with herb-flavoured soft cheese) is also a filling standby. Be wary of ordering something which perhaps sounds as if it will be meat-free, for example potato or lentil soup, but which will often contain bacon (*Speck*) or sausage.

Snacks

One of the first things you will probably notice about Berlin is its huge number of *Imbiß* fast-food stalls, offering a startling array of different foods. As well as serving *Boulette* (a kind of meatball) and *Currywurst* (sausage in a curry sauce), you can also find many ethnic fast-food outlets offering spicy *samosas*, lentil patties, and, a great favourite, *Döner Kebap*.

Table Manners

On one or two of the long tables in the beer halls (*Bierkeller*) or other big restaurants, you will occasionally see a sign proclaiming *Stammtisch* — table for regulars; the custom dates back to the medieval craft guilds. It is otherwise customary for strangers to sit together, usually after a polite query as to whether one of the empty places is *"frei."* As they sit down they wish each other *"Mahlzeit"* or *"Guten Appetit."*

It may come as a surprise that in some establishments each bread roll (*Brötchen*) is charged separately, and you are expected to keep a count of how many you eat.

Desserts

A very popular dessert is *Rote Grütze* (a compote of raspberries, cherries, and blackcurrants), generally served with *Vanillesoße* (vanilla sauce). If you really want to stretch your waisteline, indulge yourself in the German national orgy of Konditorei treats like *Schwarzwälder Kirschtorte*, the creamy cherry cake from the Black Forest; *Apfelstrudel* from Vienna, is another favourite dessert. They also love *Haselnuß-Sahnetorte* (hazelnut cream cake), *Käsekuchen* (cheesecake), and *Pflaumenkuchen* (Dresden plum cake).

What to Drink

Berlin's pubs are right at the heart of the city's social and gastronomic life.

Frederick the Great tried to produce wine at Potsdam and the resulting brew was terrible, but today many Berlin restaurants offer a first-class array of fine German wines. The red wines cannot be compared in quality to the famous whites of the Rhine and Mosel valleys but, generally speaking, the whole family of German wines is very respectable.

The most highly regarded German wines are those of the Rheingau. Among the labels to look out for are Schloß Johannisberger, Hattenheimer, Kloster Eberbacher, Steinberger, and Rüdesheimer. If you feel like celebrating, you won't go far wrong with a bottle of the champagne-like Sekt. The best of the Rhine Valley red wines come from Assmannshausen and Ingelheim.

From Rheinhessen, try the great Niersteiner Domtal and Oppenheimer. Bottled in green glass to distinguish them from the brown Rhine bottles, the Mosel wines enjoy their own delicate reputation, with the most celebrated among them being the Bernkasteler, Piesporter, Graacher, and Zeltinger.

> *Bier* is practically served everywhere. Even some American fastfood chains carry it.

Berlin's most popular drink, however, is still beer — local Schultheiss and Warburger or the best Dortmund and Bavarian brews. They are served *vom Faß*, on tap, or bottled in several varieties: *Export*, light and smooth; *Pils*, light and strong; and *Bock*, dark and rich.

During the summer months, as a refreshing surprise, try the *Berliner Weiße*, a foaming draught beer served up in a huge bowl-like glass complete with a shot of raspberry syrup or liqueur, or perhaps with *Waldmeister* (green woodruff syrup).

Berliners also like the custom of "chasing" the beer with a shot of Schnaps — any hard, clear alcohol made from potatoes, corn, barley, juniper, or another grain or berry that will distil into something to warm the cockles of your heart.

Brandy (*Weinbrand*) made in Germany is quite good, but the very strong fruit Schnaps which are distilled either from cherries (*Kirschwasser*), plums (*Zwetschgenwasser*), or raspberries (*Himbeergeist*) are very much better.

No matter what your "poison," *Prost*!

INDEX

HANDY TRAVEL TIPS

An A–Z Summary of Practical Information

Listed after many entries is the appropriate German translation, usually in the singular, plus a number of phrases that should be of help if you require assistance. The dialling code for Berlin from outside the city is 030.

A

ACCOMMODATION (See also CAMPING on page 107, and RECOMMENDED HOTELS starting on page 130)

The Berlin tourist office publishes a multilingual list with full details of accommodation. The office also provides a booking service; inquire either at the main tourist office or at Tegel Airport, or the Europa-Center (for addresses and phone numbers, see TOURIST INFORMATION OFFICES on p.126). The service is free if you write in advance; otherwise a small charge is made. It is always advisable to book at least a month ahead.

If you would like to stay in a private room, apartment, or shared house, contact one of the following organizations:

Erste Mitwohnzentrale, Sybelstr. 53, 10629 Berlin, tel. (030) 324 30 31.

Mitwohnzentrale, Ku'damm-Eck, Kurfürstendamm 227, 10719 Berlin, tel. (030) 88 30 51.

Zeitraum, Horstweg 7, 14059 Berlin, tel. (030) 325 61 81.

I'd like a single/double room. **Ich hätte gern ein Einzelzimmer/Doppelzimmer.**

YOUTH HOSTELS (*Jugendherberge*)
For information, contact the German Youth Hostel Association (Deutsches Jugendherbergswerk – DJH) at Tempelhofer Ufer 32, 10963 Berlin, tel. 262 30 24, or try one of the following:

Jugendgästehaus Berlin, Kluckstraße 3, 10785 Berlin, tel. 261 10 97; fax. 262 95 29.

Jugendgästehaus Central, Nikolsburgerstraße 2-4, 10717 Berlin, tel. 873 01 88; fax. 861 34 85.

Berlin

Jugendgästehaus Am Wannsee, Badeweg 1, 14129 Berlin, tel. 803 20 34.

Jugendherberge Ernst Reuter, Hermsdorfer Damm 48, 13467 Berlin, tel. 262 30 24; fax. 262 95 29.

Youth hostels tend to get crowded, so you should to book ahead.

AIRPORTS *(Flughafen)*

Berlin-Tegel lies about 8 km (5 miles) northwest of the city center. Taxis and buses circulate between the airport and Bahnhof Zoo in the center of the city. Bus number 109 leaves from outside the airport arrival hall at frequent and regular intervals, while bus number 128 serves northern Berlin, terminating at Wilhelmsruh. There is also an express bus, X9, from the airport to Kurfürstenstraße.

Tempelhof (Zentralflughafen) lies south of the city and connects with the center by U-Bahn line U6 (Platz der Luftbrücke) or by bus numbers 119, 184, and 341. Schönefeld Airport lies about 19 km (12 miles) south of the city center and is served by S-Bahn. Line S9 will take you to Alexanderplatz, from where bus, U- and S-Bahn connections to the rest of the city are plentiful. Alternatively, bus number 171 travels between the airport and Rudow U-Bahn station from where you can take line U7 towards the city center.

Airport information: Tegel, tel. 41 01 23 06; Tempelhof, tel. 69 51 22 88; Schönefeld, tel. 60 91 51 66

B

BICYCLE HIRE *(Fahrradverleih)*

Berlin's cyclists are safe from the traffic in their own special network of bicycle lanes. These are usually marked out by red bricks. Pedestrians should take special care to avoid walking in these lanes. Bikes are easy to rent; either look in the *Gelbe Seiten* (Yellow Pages) under FAHRRADVERLEIH, or call one of the following:

Fahrradbüro, Hauptstraße 146, 10827 Berlin, tel. 788 10 95.
Berlin By Bike, Möckernstraße 92, 10963 Berlin, tel. 216 91 77.

C

CAMPING

Four major campsites lie on the outskirts of the city:

Zeltplatz in Kladow, Krampnitzer Weg 111, 14098 Berlin,
tel. 365 27 97.
Campingplatz Haselhorst, Pulvermühlenweg, 13599 Berlin,
tel. 334 59 55.
Campingplatz Dreilinden, Kremnitz-Ufer, 14109 Berlin,
tel. 805 12 01.
Intercamping Krossinsee, Wernsdorferstraße 45, 12527 Berlin,
tel. 685 86 87.

For full information about sites, consult the guides published by the
German Automobile Club, ADAC, or the Deutscher Camping-Club:
Geisbergstraße 11, 10785 Berlin, tel. 218 60 71.

CAR HIRE (See also DRIVING).

You can arrange to hire a car immediately upon arrival at Tegel or
Schönefeld airports. Otherwise inquire at your hotel or refer to the
yellow pages of the telephone directory under AUTOVERMIETUNG for
addresses of leading firms. To hire a car you'll need a valid driving
licence held for at least one year; the minimum age is 21. Normally
a deposit is charged, but holders of major credit cards are exempt.

CHILDREN'S BERLIN

Children are reasonably well catered for in Berlin, and many of the
things you'll want to do – trips out to the Grunewald, city tours by
canal – will also appeal to young ones. Here are a few more ideas:

Museums: Children of many ages will adore the Museum of
Ethnology at Dahlem, with its exciting displays of masks, replica
ships and huts. Many of the exhibits are accessibly set out at child-
level. Older children will appreciate the interesting dioramas of the
Prehistory Museum at Schloß Charlottenburg, while the German
Technology Museum encourages hands-on activity. Domäne

Berlin

Dahlem is a re-creation of a 17th-century German village, and children can watch people at work, or admire the farm animals.

Parks and play areas: Children's play areas (*Kinderspielplatz*), with swings and climbing frames, can be found all over the city.

Zoos: Berlin has two zoos: the Zoologischer Garten near the Ku'damm and Tierpark in eastern Berlin. Both offer special features for children, including children's petting zoos, and playgrounds.

CLIMATE and CLOTHING

Average temperatures:

	J	F	M	A	M	J	J	A	S	O	N	D
°C max	2	3	8	13	19	22	25	23	20	13	7	3
°C min.	-3	-3	0	4	8	12	14	13	10	6	2	-1
°F max.	35	37	46	56	66	72	75	74	68	56	45	38
°F min.	26	26	31	39	47	53	57	56	50	42	36	29

Berlin's climate follows the continental pattern of cold, snowy winters and agreeably warm summers with low humidity. Arrange to go in late spring or summer when temperatures tend to be mild.

Clothing. Pack clothing appropriate to the season: a heavy coat in winter, lightweight garments and bathing costume in summer, raincoat, and sweater during the spring and autumn.

COMPLAINTS

If something goes wrong that you cannot take care of yourself, report the matter to the Berlin tourist office (see page 126). In hotels and restaurants, discuss any problems with the proprietor or manager.

CRIME and THEFT

Like most urban centers, Berlin's crime rate is, unfortunately, on the increase. Leave valuables in the hotel safe. Be wary of pickpockets in crowds, do not wear gold chains and other conspicuous jewelry, and don't leave objects unattended in a parked car. Report an incident to your hotel and the nearest police station. The police will give you a certificate to present to your insurance company, or to your consulate if your passport has been stolen.

It's wise to make photocopies of important documents such as passport, plane tickets, etc. – they may facilitate replacements if you lose your papers.

CUSTOMS *(Zoll)* and ENTRY FORMALITIES

For a stay of up to three months, a valid passport is sufficient for citizens of Australia, Canada, Eire, New Zealand, South Africa, the UK, and the USA. Since the introduction of the Single European Market, EU nationals may import an unlimited quantity of goods bought *tax-paid* for their own personal use. The chart below shows what you can take into Germany duty-free and, when returning home, into your own country:

Into:	Cigarettes		Cigars		Tobacco	Spirits		Wine
Australia	200	or	250	or	250g	1 *l*	or	1 *l*
Canada	200	or	50	and	900g	1.1 *l*	or	1.1*l*
N. Zealand	200	or	50	or	250g	1.1 *l*	and	4.5 *l*
S. Africa	400	and	50	and	250g	1 *l*	and	2 *l*
U.S.A.	200	and	100	and	1)	1 *l*	or	1 *l*
Within EC 2)	800	and	200	and	1kg	10 *l*	and	90 *l*

1) A reasonable quantity.
2) Guidelines for non duty-free within the EC. For the import of larger amounts you must be able to prove that the goods are for your own personal use.

Currency restrictions: There are no restrictions on the import or export of marks or any other Western currency.

D

DRIVING

To enter Germany with your car you will need:

- a national driving licence (or an international licence for those coming from the USA, Australia, New Zealand, and South Africa)

Berlin

- car registration papers
- a national identity sticker for your car
- a red warning triangle in case of breakdown
- a first-aid kit

Insurance. Third-party insurance is compulsory. Visitors from abroad, except those from EU and certain other European countries, will have to present their international certificate (Green Card) or take out third-party insurance at the border.

Driving conditions. Rush-hour traffic jams and lack of parking space make driving in central Berlin somewhat frustrating. At the beginning and end of peak holiday periods, bottlenecks tend to form on approach roads into Berlin, but traffic is generally fluid.

Drive on the right, pass on the left. Seat belts are obligatory, and that includes back-seat passengers if the car is equipped for them. If you don't wear your seat belt, insurance companies reduce compensation in the event of an accident, and you can be fined by the police.

Speed limits. The speed limit is 100 km/h (60 mph) on all open roads except for motorways and dual carriageways (divided highways), where there's no limit unless otherwise indicated. In town, speed is restricted to 50 km/h (30 mph). Cars towing caravans may not exceed 80 km/h (50 mph).

Traffic police may confiscate the car keys of persons they consider unfit to drive. Drinking and driving is a very serious offence in Germany. The permissible level of alcohol in the blood is 0.8 per mille (millilitres) – the equivalent of about two glasses of beer. Be careful, too, to stay within the speed limits; the police are getting more and more strict, and radar is used widely.

Breakdowns. For round-the-clock breakdown service call ADAC Auto Assistance, tel. 192 11.

Fuel and oil *(Benzin; Öl)*. You'll find filling stations everywhere, most of them self-service. Some are open 24 hours.

Road signs. Most road signs used in Berlin are international pictographs, but you might also come across some of the following:

Einbahnstraße	One-way street
Einordnen	Get into lane
Fußgänger	Pedestrians
Kurzparkzone	Short-term parking
Links fahren	Keep left
Parken verboten	No parking
Umleitung	Diversion (Detour)
Vorsicht	Caution
(International) Driving Licence	**(Internationaler) Führerschein**
Car Registration Papers	**Kraftfahrzeugpapiere**
Green (insurance) Card	**Grüne Versicherungskarte**

E

ELECTRIC CURRENT

Germany has 220-250 volt, 50-cycle AC. Plugs are the standard continental type, for which British and North American appliances need an adaptor.

EMBASSIES and CONSULATES *(Botschaft; Konsulat)*

Get in touch with the consulate of your home country if you lose your passport, get into trouble with the authorities or the police, or have an accident. They can issue emergency passports, give advice on obtaining money from home and provide a list of lawyers, interpreters and doctors. Phone in advance to check opening hours.

Australia: Uhlandstraße 181-3, 10623 Berlin, tel. 880 08 80.

Canada: Friedrichstraße 95, 10117 Berlin, tel. 261 11 61.

Ireland Ernst-Reuter Platz 10, 10587 Berlin, tel. 34 80 08 22.

Berlin

South Africa: Douglasstraße 9, 14163 Berlin, tel. (82 50 11.

UK: Unter den Linden 32-4, 10179 Berlin, tel. 220 24 31.

USA: Clayallee 170, 14163 Berlin, tel. 832 9233.

EMERGENCIES

(See also POLICE on page 122, and CRIME AND THEFT on page 108)
The following emergency services are available 24 hours:

Police	**110**	Fire	**112**
Ambulance	**112**	Pharmacies	**11 41**
Medical assistance	**31 00 31**		

ETIQUETTE

It is customary to shake hands when you meet someone in Germany, as it is to utter *"Guten Tag"* on entering a shop and *"Auf Wiedersehen"* when leaving. *"Tschüß"* is a more familiar way of saying goodbye. When taking leave of someone on the telephone, you should say *"Auf Wiederhören"*, literally, "Until we hear each other again." The word for "please" is *"bitte"*, also used in the sense of "you're welcome," and "thank you" is *"Danke schön."*

G

GETTING TO BERLIN

BY AIR

There are direct daily flights to Berlin from major airports all over the world, though travel from the U.S. often requires a change of planes in Frankfurt or other European capital. The cheapest fares on regular flights are APEX, which must be booked and paid for three to four weeks in advance. However, if you want a more flexible ticket, talk to a reliable travel agent. Some carriers have a special round-trip fare that can be ticketed at any time. Unless you leave things until the last minute, you will probably be able to book a charter flight or package including hotel, generally at rates and conditions even more reasonable than APEX.

BY RAIL

Berlin is well connected with other European cities by rail. Two trains depart from London for Berlin daily: from Victoria via Dover and Ostend or from Liverpool Street station by way of Harwich and the Hook of Holland. You may have to change at Hanover.

First-class travel on the Deutsche Bahn costs double the second-class fare. A supplement is charged for travel on EuroCity and InterCity trains. Children under 4 travel free in Germany, 4 to 12 year-olds pay half fare. There are two "saver" tickets, the *Sparpreis*, valid for a month, and the even cheaper *Super-Sparpreis*, valid for 10 days. If you are travelling with someone else, you can combine the saver ticket with the *Mitfahrer-Fahrpreis*, which applies for distances over 203 km. The first person pays full or saver fare, the others each pay half. Families, seniors and young people pay half fare with ID-cards valid for one year. These are obtainable at railway stations.

There are also several "go-as-you-please" passes. The Eurailpass allows unlimited travel on trains in 17 European countries including Germany, and certain ferries. It is sold only to those residing outside Europe and North Africa. European residents under 26 can buy an Inter-Rail card, valid in most European countries. It is issued for one month and enables a 50 per cent reduction on train tickets in the country of purchase and on ferries, and unlimited free travel else-where. The Deutsche Bahn also issues a tourist card, the German Rail pass, sold only to visitors. Valid for 4, 9, or 16 days, it permits unlimited travel on trains and DB Touring buses. You can buy it in Germany at major railway stations and airports, and overseas at German Rail offices.

BY ROAD

From the UK the Harwich/Hamburg crossing takes 21 hours and brings you closer to Berlin (300 km, 186 miles) than crossing from other Channel ports do.

Berlin

GUIDES and TOURS

The tourist office will put you in touch with qualified guides and interpreters for personally conducted tours or linguistic assistance.

City sightseeing tours by bus are an excellent introduction to Berlin, and most companies offer multilingual recorded commentary. Daily excursions by coach to Potsdam and the Spreewald are also available, are weekend trips to other places in Germany, including Dresden and Wittenberg. Some companies also offer nightclub tours, and the price includes a drink and entry to a show.

Most sightseeing tours depart from the Kurfürstendamm, between Rankestraße and Fasanenstraße:

Severin & Kühn Berliner Stadtrundfahrt, tel. 883 19 15. Departs Ku'damm 216, between Uhlandstraße and Fasanenstraße.

Berolina, tel. 882 20 91. Departs Ku'damm at Meinekestraße; Radisson-Plaza Hotel, Karl-Liebknecht Straße.

Berliner Bären Stadtrundfahrt (BBS), tel. 214 87 90. Departs from the Ku'damm at Rankestraße, opposite Kaiser-Wilhelm Gedächtniskirche; Alexanderplatz at the Forum Hotel.

Guide Friday, tel. 885 21 22. Departs Breitscheidplatz at Gedächtniskirche.

LANGUAGE

There is a Berlin dialect, but most people speak normal German. Although you can expect many of the people you meet in western Berlin to speak English, this will not necessarily be the case in the east, and a little German will go a long way towards breaking the ice.

The Berlitz phrasebook GERMAN FOR TRAVELLERS covers most of the situations you are likely to encounter in Germany, and the German-English/English-German pocket dictionary contains a special menu-reader supplement and a short grammar section. For a list of useful expressions, see the cover of this guide.

LAUNDRY and DRY-CLEANING

Having your laundry washed or cleaned by the hotel is the quickest and most convenient method, but prices are high, so it's worth seeking out a *Waschsalon* (launderette) or *Wäscherei* (laundry). Dry-cleaning usually takes two days. Some cleaners offer a quick service *(Schnellreinigung)* which takes a minimum of two hours and is slightly more expensive.

LOST PROPERTY

Berlin's central lost-property office *(Zentrales Fundbüro)* is at Platz der Luftbrücke 6, 12099 Berlin, tel. 69 90. If you know where you left your property, call the *Fundbüro* of the service concerned. If it was on the public transport, contact the BVG at Lorenzweg 5, 12099 Berlin, tel. 751 80 21.

For anything lost in a post office or telephone box, inquire at the main post office, Bahnhof Zoo, tel. 313 97 99.

M

MAPS

Excellent free street maps *(Stadtplan)* are available at the tourist offices, some banks, car-hire firms and bigger hotels.

MEDICAL CARE

Ask your insurance company before leaving home if you are covered for medical treatment in Germany. Visitors who are not reimbursed for medical bills abroad can take out a short-term holiday policy before setting out. Citizens of EU countries may use the German Health Services for medical treatment. Ask for the requisite form at your local Health and Social Security Office.

In the event of accident or serious illness, call for an ambulance, **112**, or ask the medical emergency service, tel. 31 00 31, to recommend a doctor.

Berlin

Pharmacies are open during normal shopping hours. At night and on Sundays and holidays, all chemists display the address of the nearest one open. For emergencies, call **11 41**.

MONEY MATTERS

Currency. Germany's monetary unit is the *Deutsche Mark* (DM). The mark is divided into 100 *Pfennigs* (Pf.).

Coins: 1, 2, 5, 10, and 50 Pf. and DM 1, 2 and 5.
Notes: DM 5, 10, 20, 50, 100, 200, 500 and 1,000.

Banking hours are usually from 9AM to 12PM Monday to Friday. Most banks remain open from 1PM to 3PM three afternoons a week, and from 2PM to 6PM two afternoons a week; however days vary, so you'll have to check posted notices. Branches in the big stores operate during normal shopping hours. The currency exchange office of the Deutsche Verkehrsbank in Bahnhof Zoo is open from 8.30AM to 10PM Monday to Friday, and from 8AM to 7PM at weekends.

Changing money. Foreign currency can be changed at ordinary banks *(Bank)*, savings banks *(Sparkasse)* and currency exchange offices *(Wechselstube)*. Hotels, travel agencies, and Berlin's central post office also have exchange facilities, but rates are less favourable. The same is true of currency and traveller's cheques changed in shops or restaurants.

Credit cards, traveller's cheques, Eurocheques. Credit cards are accepted in most hotels, restaurants, and large shops. Eurocheques and traveller's cheques, supported by identification, are accepted by many establishments. Cash is usually preferred in eastern Berlin.

I want to change some pounds/ dollars.	**Ich möchte Pfund/ Dollars wechseln.**
Can I pay with this credit card?	**Kann ich mit dieser Kreditkarte zahlen?**

PLANNING YOUR BUDGET

The following list will give you some idea of what prices to expect in Berlin, but as we can never keep up with inflation, they can only be considered approximate.

Airport transfer. City bus to Bahnhof Zoo DM 3.60, taxi from Tegel DM 25, from Schönefeld DM 55.

Babysitters. DM 15-20 per hour.

Camping. *Tent:* DM 5.50 per person per night; *caravan (trailer)*: DM 7.50 per person per night.

Car hire. *VW Polo* DM 70 per day, DM 0.70 per km., DM 150 per weekend (Friday noon-Monday 9am) up to 1,500km free, DM 700 per week with unlimited mileage.

Entertainment. *Cinema* DM 8-12, *theater* DM 15-60, *discotheque* DM 20-50, *nightclub* DM 25-200.

Food and drink. 1 kilo of bread DM 4-6, 250g DM 2-2.60, 100g German sausage DM 2.50, 100g smoked ham DM 2.60-3, 100g meat or vegetable salad DM 1.60-4, 100g cheese DM 1.80-3, beer (1/2 litre) DM 2.50.

Hairdressers. *Man's* haircut DM 35-60. *Woman's* haircut DM 30-90.

Hotels (double room per night). Luxury class DM 350-475, first class DM 220-350, medium range DM 120-220, budget class DM 80-115.

Meals and drinks. Breakfast DM 8-25, lunch or dinner in fairly good establishment DM 30-70, bottle of wine (German) DM 35-60, beer (small bottle) DM 3.50-6, soft drink (small bottle) DM 3-5, coffee DM 2.50-4.

Museums. DM 4-6; *Tageskarte:* DM 8; *Sammelkarte* (Schloß Charlottenburg): DM 8; reductions for children and students.

Berlin

Public transport. BVG: single ticket DM 3.70, children DM 2.50; *Ku'damm-Ticket:* DM 2.00; *Sammelkarte* (four trips): DM 12.50, children DM 8.50; Berlin Ticket (valid for 30 hours): DM 15; 7-day ticket (valid from Monday to Sunday): DM 40; *Umweltkarte* (1 month): DM 89.

Sightseeing. City Tour (2½ hours) DM 30, Big Berlin Tour (3 hours) DM 39, Super Berlin Tour (incl. stop at Pergamon Museum) DM 45, Spreewald tour (6 hours) DM 54, Potsdam tour (7 hours, incl. lunch) DM 95.

Taxis. Initial charge DM 3.80, plus DM 1.93 per km (before 11PM), DM 2.10 (after 11PM).

NEWSPAPERS and MAGAZINES *(Zeitungen; Zeitschriften)*

Major American, British and other European newspapers and magazines are on sale at newsagents and kiosks in the city center, as well as at big hotels and at the airports.

O

OPENING HOURS

The opening times and telephone numbers of the major museums are listed below alphabetically by area. Note that many museums are free on Sundays and public holidays.

Berlin-Mitte

Brecht-Weigel-Haus, Chausseestraße125, tel. 282 99 16. Open Tuesday to Friday 10-11.30AM, Saturday 9.30AM-1.30PM, Thursday 5-6.30PM. Guided tours are every half-hour with a maximum of 8 people per tour.

Deutsches Historisches Museum, Unter den Linden 2, tel. 21 50 20. Open daily except Wednesday, 10AM-6PM.

Märkisches Museum, Am Köllnischen Park 5, tel. 270 05 14. Open Tuesday to Sunday 10AM-6PM.

Otto-Nagel-Haus, Märkisches Ufer 16, tel. 279 14 02. Open Sunday to Thursday 9AM-5PM.

Charlottenburg

Ägyptisches Museum (Egyptian Museum), Schloßstraße 70, tel. 32 09 12 61; disabled visitors should ring in advance. Open 9AM-5PM Monday to Thursday, 10AM-5PM weekends, closed Friday.

Antikensammlung Charlottenburg, Sophie-Charlottestraße 17-18, tel. 3 21 70 11. Open 9AM-5PM Monday to Friday, 9AM-6PM Wednesday.

Bröhan Museum, Schloßstraße 1a, tel. 3 21 40 29; disabled visitors should register in advance. Open 10AM-6PM Tuesday to Sunday and public holidays.

Haus der Zeitgenössischen Kunst, Schloßstraße 1, tel. 32 09 11. Open Tuesday to Friday, 9AM-5PM, weekends 10AM-5PM.

Käthe-Kollwitz Museum, Fasanenstraße 24, tel. 882 52 10; disabled access to ground floor only. Open daily except Tuesday, 11AM-6PM.

Museum für Vor- und Frühgeschichte (Museum for Primeval and Early History), Spandauer Damm 22, tel. 32 09 12 33; limited facilities for disabled visitors. Open Monday to Thursday 9AM-5PM, weekends 10AM-5PM.

Schloß Charlottenburg, Luisenplatz, tel. 32 09 11; ground floor access only to disabled visitors. Open Tuesday to Friday 9AM-5PM, weekends 10AM-5PM.

Berlin

Dahlem

Botanischer Garten/Botanisches Museum, Königin-Luise-Straße 6-8 and entrance on Unter den Eichen, tel. 83 00 61 27. *Garden:* open daily 9AM-dusk; *museum:* Tuesday to Sunday 10-5PM.

Brücke Museum, Bussardsteig 9, tel. 831 20 29. Open daily except Tuesday 11AM-5PM.

Gemäldegalerie (Picture Gallery), Arnimallee 23-7, tel. 830 11; disabled visitors should phone in advance. Open Tuesday to Friday 9AM-5PM, weekends 10AM-5PM.

Museen für Außereuropäische Kulturen (Museums of non-European Cultures), Lansstraße 8, tel. 830 13 82. Open Tuesday to Friday 9AM-5PM, weekends 10AM-5PM.

Museum für Völkerkunde (Museum of Ethnology), Lansstraße 8, tel. 830 12 28; disabled access to most parts of the museum. Open Tuesday to Friday 9AM-5PM, weekends 10AM-5PM.

Kreuzberg

Berlin Museum, Lindenstraße 14, tel. 25 86 28 39. Open 10AM-8PM Tuesday to Sunday, though check precise times when museum opens after extensive renovations are completed in 1998.

Martin-Gropius-Bau, Stresemannstraße 110, tel. 25 48 60; disabled visitors should register on arrival. Open Tuesday to Sunday 10AM-8PM.

Deutsches Technikmuseum Berlin (German Technology Museum), Trebbiner Straße 9, tel. 25 48 40. Open Tuesday to Friday 9AM-5.30PM, weekends 10AM-6PM.

Topographie des Terrors (Topography of Terror), Stresemannstraße 110, tel. 25 48 67 03. Open daily 10AM-6PM, tours by appointment.

Museumsinsel

All Museumsinsel museums open Tuesday to Sunday, 9AM-5PM. Tel. for all is 20 90 5555.

Altes Museum (Old Museum), Bodestraße 1-3, entrance on Lustgarten.

Bode-Museum, Bodestraße 1-3, entrance from Monbijoubrücke; disabled access from service entrance at Alte Nationalgalerie.

Nationalgalerie (Old National Gallery), Bodestraße 1-3, entrance on Monbijoubrücke; disabled visitors should report to service entrance.

Pergamonmuseum, Bodestraße 1-3.

Nikolaiviertel

Ephraim-Palais, Poststraße 16, tel. 23 80 900; tours by appointment; disabled visitors should register on arrival. Open Tuesday to Saturday 10AM-6PM.

Nikolaikirche, Nikolaiplatz, tel. 23 80 90 84; disabled visitors should ring in advancet. Open Tuesday to Sunday 9AM-6PM.

Tiergarten

Bauhaus-Archiv-Museum für Gestaltung, Klingelhöferstraße 13-14, tel. 254 00 20. Open daily except Tuesday 10AM-5PM.

Hamburger Bahnhof Museum für Gegenwart, Invalidenstraße 50, tel. 397 83 40. Open Tuesday to Friday 9AM-5PM, weekends 10AM-5PM.

Kunstgewerbemuseum (Arts and Crafts Museum), Matthäikirchplatz, tel. 266 29 02. Open Tuesday to Friday 9AM-5PM, weekends 10AM-5PM.

Musikinstrumentenmuseum (Musical Instruments Museum), Tiergartenstraße 1, tel. 25 48 10. Open Tuesday to Friday 9AM–5PM, weekends 10AM-5PM; tours 11AM every Saturday; Wurlitzer Organ presentation first Saturday of every month.

Neue Nationalgalerie (New National Gallery), Potsdamer Straße 50, tel. 266 26 51. Open Tuesday to Friday 9AM-5PM, weekends 10AM-5PM.

Reichstag, Platz der Republik. Open 10AM-5PM every day except Monday.

P

PHOTOGRAPHY and VIDEO

All makes of film are easily found and can be developed overnight or even within an hour. Airport security machines use X-rays which can fog your film after more than four scannings. Video cassettes are also widely available, though you must make sure they are compatible with your equipment back home.

POLICE *(Polizei)*

Germany's police wear green uniforms. You'll see them on white motorcycles or in green-and-white cars or vans. The police emergency number is **110**. Berlin's central police station *(Polizeipräsidium)* is at Platz der Luftbrücke 6, 12099 Berlin.

POST OFFICES

Mail boxes are yellow, and you should deposit non-local letters or cards in the slot marked *Andere Richtungen.* Berlin's central post office *(Postamt)* is located in Bahnhof Zoo. It stays open 24 hours a day and handles mail, telegrams, public telex, fax, and telephone services. You can have mail directed to you here: c/o Hauptpostlagernd, Postamt 120, Bahnhof Zoo, 10585 Berlin.

Remember to take your passport or identity card when you go to collect your mail.

The post office at Tegel Airport is open daily from 7AM to 9PM. Other branch offices of Germany's Bundespost generally open

Monday to Friday from 8AM to 6PM, and until noon on Saturday. In eastern Berlin, 24-hour mail service is available at the Hauptbahnhof, Straße der Pariser Kommune 8-12.

Faxes can be sent from public copy centers and from many hotels.

PUBLIC HOLIDAYS *(Feiertag)*

The chart below shows the public holidays celebrated in Berlin, when shops, banks, official departments, and many restaurants are closed. If a holidays falls on a Thursday, many people take the Friday off, too, to make a long weekend.

On 24 December (Christmas Eve), shops stay open until noon, but most restaurants, theaters, cinemas, and concert halls are closed.

1 January	*Neujahr*	New Year's Day
1 May	*Tag der Arbeit*	Labour Day
3 October	*Tag der Einheit*	Reunification Day
25, 26 December	*Weihnachten*	Christmas
Movable dates:	*Karfreitag*	Good Friday
	Ostermontag	Easter Monday
	Christi Himmelfahrt	Ascension Day
	Pfingstmontag	Whit Monday
	Buß- und Bettag	Day of Prayer and Repentance (3rd Wednesday in November)

PUBLIC TRANSPORT

Berlin is served by an efficient network of buses, trams, U-Bahn (underground railway), S-Bahn (suburban railway) and Regionalbahn (regional railway) administered by the *Berliner Verkehrsbetriebe,* or BVG for short. The U-Bahn comprises nine lines covering the inner city and many outlying districts, while the bus service reaches virtually every corner of Berlin. The S-Bahn provides an efficient link to places further afield such as the

Berlin

Grunewald, Wannsee, Potsdam and Köpenick. Plans are afoot to extend the tram network, currently operating in eastern Berlin only.

The **U-Bahn** operates from about 4.30AM to about 1AM. Lines U1 and U9 travel all night on Friday and Saturday.

Buses run round the clock, though the skeleton night services operating between 1AM and 4AM are less frequent and cover slightly different routes. Bus stops are easily recognizable by a yellow sign marked with a green 'H'.

U-Bahn stations are marked by a white 'U' on a blue background, and S-Bahn stations by a white 'S' on a green background.

Tickets are interchangeable between trains, buses, and trams, entitling you to free transfers for up to 2 hours. Be sure to have plenty of small change for the orange vending machines which distribute tickets at the U-Bahn stations and most bus stops. A few of them also take banknotes. If the machine rejects a coin try with another (they tend to be unpredictable). Stamp your ticket in one of the red machines *(Entwerter)* on station platforms and in buses. To buy a ticket on the bus itself, it's best to have the exact money ready, though drivers will give change. You can also buy a ticket valid for four rides *(Sammelkarte)*, or the 30-hour Berlin Ticket which can be used on all BVG lines without restriction, including certain ferries.

Long-distance buses serve many destinations in Germany. Coaches depart from the central bus station *(Zentraler Omnibusbahnhof)* near the Funkturm in Messedamm, tel. 180 28.

R

RADIO and TV *(Radio, Fernsehen)*

You can easily pick up the BBC World Service or the Voice of America. As for television, there are two commercial-free national channels – ARD and ZDF, plus a regional station, SFB, and several private and cable stations.

RELIGION

A complete list of churches, synagogues, mosques, and temples can be obtained from the tourist office (see page 126). You should always keep your head covered when in a Jewish synagogue or cemetery.

TAXIS

Berlin taxis are mostly beige Mercedes. Catch one at a rank, at busy locations such as the Ku'damm/Joachimstaler Straße intersection, or hail a driver. You can also book in advance through your hotel or by phoning one of the following numbers:

26 10 26   **690 22**   **21 02 02**

TELEPHONES

International calls can be made from phone booths marked "International." Telephone lines from eastern Berlin have been extensively modernized and long-distance calls should be as straightforward as from the western areas of the city. Area code numbers have recently been changed, so if you are having difficulty obtaining a number, try directory enquiries. Phone cards *(Telefonkarte)* are widely used and they can be obtained at any post office. Communications within Germany and to neighbouring countries are cheaper from 6PM-8AM weekdays and all day Saturday and Sunday. Rates for Canada and the US are cut between midnight and noon. Some useful numbers:

Enquiries: domestic 011 88, international 001 18

Operator: domestic 010, international 0010

Go in person to a post office or phone in messages from your hotel or any private telephone (dial 1131).

Berlin

TIME DIFFERENCES

Germany follows Central European Time (GMT + 1):

New York	London	**Berlin**	Jo'burg	Sydney	Auckland
6AM	11AM	**noon**	noon	8PM	10PM

TIPPING

Since a service charge is normally included in hotel and restaurant bills, tipping is not obligatory. However it's appropriate to give something to porters, cloakroom attendants, etc, for their services. The chart below gives some suggestions as to how much to leave.

Hairdresser/barber	10-15%
Lavatory attendant	DM 0.50-1
Maid, per week	DM 5-10
Porter, per bag	DM 1-2
Taxi driver	10%
Tourist guide	DM 1-5
Waiter	(optional) 5%

TOILETS

Public toilets are readily found. Always have 10-Pfennig coins ready in case the door has a slot machine. Toilets may be labelled with symbols of a man or a woman or the initials WC. Otherwise *Herren* (Gentlemen) or *Damen* (Ladies) are indicated.

TOURIST INFORMATION OFFICES

The German National Tourist Board – Deutsche Zentrale für Tourismus e. V. (DZT) – can give you information on when to go, where to stay and what to see in Berlin. The headquarters is at: Beethovenstraße 69, D-6000 Frankfurt am Main, tel. (069) 757 20.

The national tourist organization also maintains offices in many countries throughout the world:

Canada: 175 Bloor Street, Toronto, Ontario M4W 3R8, tel. (416) 968-1570.

UK: 65 Curzon Street, London W1Y 7PE, tel. (0891) 600 100.

USA: 122 East 42nd Street, 52nd floor, New York, NY 10168, tel. (212) 661-7200; 11766 Wilshire Boulevard, Suite 750, Los Angeles, CA 90025; tel. (310) 575-9799.

Tourist information offices in Berlin:

Tourismus Marketing: Europa-Center, Budapester Straße, 10787 Berlin, tel. 262 60 31; open Monday to Saturday 9AM-9PM.

Brandenburger Tor, tel. 25 00 25; open daily 9:30AM-6PM.

Verkehrsamt im Flughafen Tegel: Main Hall, tel. 41 01 31 45; pen daily 8AM-11PM.

In addition to free maps, lists and brochures, Berlin's tourist offices offer a hotel booking service. You'll find listings of sights, hotels, and restaurants at the Berlin Tourismus web site, http:\\www.berlin.de.

TRAVELLERS WITH DISABILITIES

Many efforts have been made to improve the city's accessibility to travellers with disabilities. Maps of the city transport network show which U- and S-Bahn stations have wheelchair facilities. Buses have wide rear doors and some have lifts and safety straps for wheelchairs. Many museums have wheelchair access, lifts and specially adapted toilet facilities. *Berlin Programm*, and *Berlin, Das Magazin* lists which of them cater for visitors with disabilites, although it is always best to phone in advance. For more information, contact Berlin tourist office (see page 126).

W

WATER

Tap water is perfectly safe to drink; only rarely will you see the warning *Kein Trinkwasser* (not suitable for drinking).

WEIGHTS AND MEASURES

Length

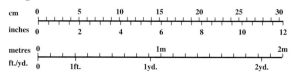

Weight

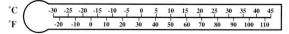

Temperature

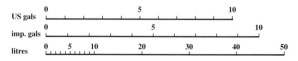

Fluid measures

Distance

km	0	1	2	3	4	5	6	8	10	12	14	16
miles	0	½	1	1½	2	3	4	5	6	7	8	9	10

A SELECTION OF HOTELS AND RESTAURANTS

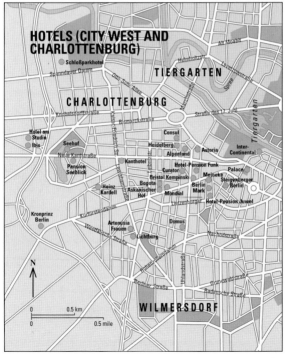

HOTELS (CITY WEST AND CHARLOTTENBURG)

Recommended Hotels

We give below a selection of hotels in four price categories, grouped in the following areas: Berlin City, west; Charlottenburg; Kreuzberg; Berlin City, east; and Potsdam. You are advised to book your accommodation well in advance, either through your travel agent or directly with the hotel. We have included phone numbers and, where possible, fax numbers too.

Hotels in the east have begun to open up since reunification, although you shouldn't expect standards of service and quality as high as those in the west. However, the situation will only improve with time, and some of the better hotels in Mitte are superbly situated for exploring many of the city's major sights.

Breakfast is normally included in the price of the room, but some of the more expensive establishments ask for a supplementary charge. As a basic guide to prices, we have used the following symbols (for a double room with bath and usually breakfast):

✪	below 190 DM
✪✪	190-220 DM
✪✪✪	220-350 DM
✪✪✪✪	above 350 DM

The telephone country code for Germany is 49 and the city code for Berlin is 30.

Berlin City, west

Artemisia Frauenhotel ✪✪ *Brandenburgische Str. 18, 10707 Berlin; tel. 87 '89 05; fax 861 86 53*. Small, hotel garni for women only, with facilities for children.

Askanischer Hof ✪✪✪ *Kurfürstendamm 53, 107807 Berlin; tel. 881 80 33/34; fax 881 72 06*. A small, family-run hotel garni set in an excellent location. Delightful 1900s atmosphere and a very friendly reception. Children welcome.

Berlin Mark Hotel ✪✪✪ *Meinekestr. 18-19, 10719 Berlin; tel. 88 00 2; fax 88 00 28 04*. 233 rooms. Well-situated family hotel with wheelchair facilities. It also has its own bistro with terrace.

Bristol-Hotel Kempinski ✪✪✪ *Kurfürstendamm 27, 10719 Berlin; tel. 88 43 40; fax 883 60 75*. A large, luxurious international hotel boasting some excellent facilities: conference rooms, several restaurants, solarium, sauna, babysitting services, indoor swimming pool. The sound-proofed rooms are very comfortable and pleasingly furnished.

Concept Hotel ✪✪✪ *Grolmanstr. 41-43, 10623 Berlin; tel. 88 42 60; fax 88 42 65 00*. In a quiet location near Savignyplatz, this elegant hotel offers 100 tastefully furnished rooms, as well as a sauna, solarium, and bar.

Grand Hotel Esplanade ✪✪✪✪ *Lützowufer 15, 10785 Berlin; tel. 25 47 82; fax 265 11 71*. Some 402 elegantly furnished bedrooms and a delightful cocktail bar on the ground floor. No charge for children up to 12 sharing their parents' room. Resident doctor; library with 4,000 art books. Breakfast is extra, however.

Hotel Astoria ✪✪✪ *Fasanenstr. 2, 10623 Berlin; tel. 312 40 67; fax 312 50 27*. Hotel garni with 33 rooms in agreeable central location. Special rates are available for children under 12. Services offered include babysitting facilities, airport bus and hotel yacht.

Hotel Bogota ✪-✪✪ *Schlüterstr. 45, 10707 Berlin; tel. 881 50 01; fax 883 58 87.* This hotel is pleasantly situated just off the Ku'damm and offers a range of rooms, most with showers and toilets. The friendly staff also speak English.

Hotel Consul ✪✪ *Knesebeckstr. 8-9, 10623 Berlin; tel. 31 10 60; fax 312 20 60.* The hotel is in the process of renovation, and offers large rooms with a comfortable guest lounge.

Hotel Domus ✪ *Uhlandstr. 49, 10719 Berlin; tel. 88 20 41, fax 882 04 10.* 72 rooms. Centrally located hotel garni.

Hotel Eden ✪✪✪ *Sächsische Str. 70, 10707 Berlin; tel. 882 20 66; fax 882 57 61.* Hotel garni with traditional atmosphere. No charge for children under 12 sharing parents' room.

Hotel Heidelberg ✪ *Knesebeckstr. 15, 10623 Berlin; tel. 313 01 03; fax 313 58 70.* 40 rooms. Family-run hotel garni; quietly situated near Savignyplatz. Facilities for children. Airport bus.

Hotel Inter-Continental ✪✪✪✪ *Budapester Str. 2, 10787 Berlin; tel. 2 60 20; fax 260 28 07 60.* Large, modern hotel, with two restaurants, indoor swimming pool, sauna and excellent facilities for business travellers. View over the Tiergarten. Breakfast is extra.

Hotel Kronprinz Berlin ✪✪ *Kronprinzendamm 1, 10711 Berlin; tel. 89 60 30; fax 8 93 12 15.* An attractive hotel situated in an old Berlin mansion. Some rooms have balconies, and the small garden is sometimes the venue for sculpture exhibitions.

Hotel Palace ✪✪✪✪ *Europa Center, 10789 Berlin; tel. 25 020; fax 262 65 77*. Some 322 rooms. This conveniently situated hotel underwent extensive restoration during mid-1993, and offers spacious, well-fitted rooms in addition to conference facilities and its own restaurant. Breakfast is extra.

Hotel-Pension Funk ✪✪ *Fasanenstr. 69, 10719 Berlin; tel. 882 71 93; fax 883 33 29*. This small hotel has 15 ample rooms, though not all have showers. Situated in one of the most delightful streets off the busy Kurfürstendamm.

Mondial ✪✪✪ *Kurfürstendamm 47, 10707 Berlin; tel. 88 41 10; fax 88 41 11 50*. Comfortable rooms and friendly service are just two assets. Facilities for disabled visitors.

Steigenberger Berlin ✪✪✪✪ *Los-Angeles-Platz 1, 10789 Berlin; tel. 212 70; fax 212 71 17*. Large, modern hotel in an excellent central location, with its own conference facilities, plus a sauna and solarium.

Charlottenburg

Hotel am Studio ✪-✪✪ *Kaiserdamm 80-81, 14057 Berlin; tel. 30 20 81; fax 301 95 78*. Hotel garni with 77 pleasant bedrooms. Special rates are available for children.

Hotel Heinz Kardell ✪✪ *Gervinusstr. 24, 10629 Berlin; tel. 324 10 66; fax 324 97 10*. 32 rooms. Near Charlottenburg S-Bahn station. Quiet, family-run. International restaurant; special diets on request.

Hotel Seehof ✪✪✪-✪✪✪✪ *Lietzensee-Ufer 11, 14057 Berlin; tel. 32 00 2; fax 32 00 22 51*. Some 77 rooms. Attractive, modern hotel on the shores of the Lietzensee, with conference facilities, sauna, lift and restaurant. Breakfast is extra.

Berlin

Kanthotel ✪✪ *Kantstr. 111, 10627 Berlin; tel. 32 30 20; fax 324 09 52.* 55 rooms. Family-run hotel garni. Babysitting services, rooms for disabled guests, conference facilities. Special rates for children and at weekends.

Schloßparkhotel ✪✪ *Heubnerweg 2a, 14059 Berlin; tel. 322 40 61; fax 325 88 61.* 39 rooms. Situated in a quiet location near Charlottenburg Palace gardens, the hotel offers a swimming pool as well as conference facilities.

Kreuzberg

Antares Hotel am Potsdamer Platz ✪✪ *Stresemannstr. 97, 10963 Berlin; tel. 25 41 60; fax 261 50 27.* 85 rooms. Quiet, modern hotel garni near Anhalter Bahnhof. Conference facilities. There's no charge for children under 12 sharing their parents' room.

Hotel Transit ✪ *Hagelberger Str. 53-54, 10965 Berlin; tel. 785 50 51; fax 785 96 19.* Inexpensive hotel with young atmosphere. Dormitory accommodation is available for travellers on a tight budget. Friendly staff speak good English.

Riehmers Hofgarten ✪✪ *Yorckstr. 83, 10965 Berlin; tel. 78 10 11; fax 786 60 59.* 38 rooms. Comfortable hotel garni in a historic building near leafy Viktoria Park, with restaurant, lift and conference facilities. The hotel is excellently situated for exploring Kreuzberg and Mitte.

Berlin City, east

Berlin Hilton ✪✪✪✪ *Mohrenstr. 30, 10117 Berlin; tel. 20 230; fax 20 23 42 69.* 370 rooms. Originally known as the Dom, this modern hotel was taken over by the Hilton in 1991. It is situated on the splendidly historic site near Gendarmenmarkt, and offers excellent rooms as well as 6 restaurants, sauna, swimming pool and squash court.

Hotel Luisenhof ✪✪ *Köpenicker Str. 92, 10119 Berlin; tel. 241 59 06; fax 279 29 83.* Situated in a charmingly restored nineteenth-century town house, this hotel is ideally located for exploring the museums and other cultural attractions around Mitte. Useful services available include fax and photocopying facilities, and rooms are equipped with TV, radio and minibar.

Hotel Märkischer Hof ✪ *Linienstr. 133, 10115 Berlin; tel. 282 71 55; fax 282 43 31.* Very conveniently situated near Friedrichstraße, this family-run hotel is welcoming and friendly, and the comfortable rooms are agreeably furnished. Services include conference facilities, TV, radio and telephone in all rooms, and a guest lounge.

Hotel Unter den Linden ✪✪✪ *Unter den Linden 14, 10117 Berlin; tel. 23 81 10; fax 23 81 11 00.* 324 rooms. Comfortable and attractively furnished, though the rooms are a bit on the small side. The welcome is friendly, and the hotel is excellently situated for Museumsinsel.

Grand Hotel Berlin ✪✪✪✪ *Friedrichstr. 158-164, 10117 Berlin; tel. 202 70; fax 20 27 34 19.* 380 rooms. Exquisitely furnished in tasteful period decor, this lovely hotel dominates the corner of Unter den Linden and Friedrichstraße and is very well situated for the museums on Museumsinsel. The hotel has ten bars and restaurants and a sun patio. Breakfast is extra.

Berlin

Maritim Pro Arte ✪✪✪✪ *Friedrichstr. 151, 10117 Berlin; tel. 203 35; fax 20 33 42 09.* 3403 rooms, recently refurbished. The hotel has four restaurants, all modern amenities, including facilities for disabled guests, and is well situated for excursions to Unter den Linden and the Brandenburg Gate. Breakfast is extra.

SAAS Hotel Berlin ✪✪✪ *Karl-Liebknecht-Str. 5, 10178 Berlin; tel. 238 28; fax 238 27590.* Modern hotel with 540 rooms, all newly refurbished. Facilities include four restaurants, sauna, conference center, licensed bar, and a television in each room. Breakfast is extra.

Victoria Hotelschiff ✪ *Puschkinallee 16-17, 12435 Berlin; tel. 53 33 70; fax 53 33 72 22.* Single cabins and double rooms in an old river boat. Hotel has also a restaurant with wintergarden. Breakfast is extra.

Potsdam

Hotel Mercure Potsdam ✪✪ *Lange Brücke, 14467 Potsdam; tel. (0331) 27 22; fax 29 34 96.* This modern, high-rise hotel is located within easy reach of the town. The hotel offers 184 comfortable, though rather functional rooms, in addition to well-equipped conference facilities, a bar, and restaurant. The restaurant will cater to special diets on request. Good views over the town and the River Havel.

Travel Hotel Schloß Cecilienhof ✪✪✪ *Neuer Garten, 14469 Potsdam; tel. (0331) 3 70 50; fax 29 24 98.* Situated in the wing of the palace where the Potsdam Agreement was signed, the hotel has a comfortable country house hotel atmosphere. A car is essential.

Recommended Restaurants

With scores of restaurants to choose from in Berlin, where do you start? To give you some guidance, we have made a selection covering a range of locations, types of cuisine and prices. However, restaurants are continually changing, particularly in eastern Berlin where, as yet, standards of quality and service do not always match up to those of the west. Therefore, we recommend that you listen to local advice, as no list can be completely up-to-date.

There are very few really low-cost eating establishments in the city, although you will find several bargain pizza, pasta and burger joints. Look out for set menus, which are offered by most restaurants — they usually represent good value for money. As a basic guide, we have used the following symbols to give an idea of the price for a three-course meal, for one, including a service charge of 15%, but excluding wine (drinks, especially wine, will add considerably to the final bill):

✪	below 50 DM
✪✪	50-70 DM
✪✪✪	above 70 DM

Many Berlin restaurants close for one or two days a week, and also around Christmas and New Year and for a few weeks in summer. It's advisable to phone in advance, to make sure the restaurant is open.

Berlin City, west

Café Kranzler ✪✪ *Kurfürstendamm 18, 10719 Berlin; tel. 882 69 11.* Smart bourgeois atmosphere overlooking the lively Ku'damm (see also page 33). This is where Berliners go to be seen. Open from 8AM until midnight.

Berlin

Café Möhring ✪✪ *Kurfürstendamm 213, 10719 Berlin; tel. 881 20 75.* Once the haunt of intellectuals and politicians, now an institution in its own right, with elegant décor and soothing classical music. Open daily 7AM to 9PM, weekends to 11PM.

Florian ✪✪ *Grolmanstr. 52, 10623 Berlin; tel. 313 91 84.* Noisy, intellectual chic in the fashionable area around Savignyplatz. Reservations advised. Open 6PM to 3AM daily.

Fofi's ✪✪ *Rathaustr. 25, 10178 Berlin; tel. 242 34 35.* A regular clientele testifies to the superb Italian-Greek cuisine. Open 7:30PM to 1AM daily.

Hard Rock Café ✪ *Meinekestr. 21, 10719 Berlin; tel. 88 46 20.* Loud but well-loved by Americans seeking home from home. Authentic hamburgers and there's always a lively crowd. Open 12 noon to 2AM daily.

Hardtke ✪ *Meinekestr. 27, 10719 Berlin; tel. 881 98 27.* Traditional Berlin specialities including home-made sausage, in a lively German atmosphere. Open daily 10AM to midnight.

Istanbul ✪-✪✪ *Knesebeckstr. 77, 10623 Berlin; tel. 883 27 77.* Extensive menu offering a choice of delicious Turkish dishes, including vegetarian starters. Open daily noon to midnight.

Kashmir Palace ✪✪✪ *Marburger Str. 14, 10789 Berlin; tel. 214 28 40.* Sumptuous northern Indian food in an opulent setting. Open noon to 3PM and 6PM to midnight daily.

Kempinski-Grill ✪✪✪ *Kurfürstendamm 27, 10719 Berlin; tel. 88 43 40.* Luxuriously renovated, famed more for décor and location than for overrated cuisine. Open 1-3PM and 6PM to midnight daily.

Lutter & Wegner ✪✪ *Schlüterstr. 55, 10629 Berlin ; tel. 881 34 40.* An elegant Berlin institution which has been going strong since 1811, and is popular with young and old. Jazz adds to the charm. Open daily from 6PM until 3AM.

Restaurant am Fasanenplatz ✪✪-✪✪✪ *Fasanenstr. 42, 10719 Berlin; tel. 883 97 23.* Reservations are recommended for this friendly restaurant with a relaxed atmosphere specializing in refined German cuisine. Open from noon to 2PM, and 5:30-11:30 PM Sunday. Closed Monday.

Shell ✪ *Knesebeckstr. 22, 10623 Berlin; tel. 312 83 10.* Located in a former petrol station, this simple restaurant is popular with locals because of its superb food and keen prices. Cuisine is international and there is a good range of vegetarian dishes. Service can be slow, so don't come here if you're in a hurry. Open Monday to Saturday 9AM to 1AM, from 10AM Sundays and holidays.

Wintergarten ✪ *Fasanenstr. 23, 10719 Berlin; tel. 882 54 14.* This haven of peace is situated in the Literaturhaus villa and is the perfect place to collect your thoughts after visiting the Käthe- Kollwitz museum nearby. The salon at the back is ideal on sunny days. Open from 9:30AM until 1AM.

Charlottenburg

Alt Luxemburg ✪✪ *Windscheidstr. 31, 10627 Berlin; tel. 323 87 30.* Excellent, traditional cuisine served in a suitably bourgeois décor. Reservations are strongly advised. Open Monday to Saturday from 7PM to 1AM.

Angkor ✪✪ *Seelingstr. 34-36, 14059 Berlin; tel. 325 59 94.* Exquisite Cambodian cuisine served in refined ambience. Reservations advisable. Open weekdays 6PM until 11PM, weekends noon to 11PM.

Ax Bax ✪ *Leibnizstr. 34, 10625 Berlin; tel. 313 85 94.* Traditional German and Austrian dishes are served in sober surroundings by very smart Viennese waiters. Reservation advisable. Open daily (except Monday) from 7PM until 3AM.

Der Ägypter ✪ *Kantstr. 26, 10623 Berlin; tel. 313 92 30.* Restaurant which specializes in wholesome and reasonably priced Egyptian cuisine. Portions are extremely copious and vegetarians are well catered for. Open daily from 5PM to 1AM.

Paris-Bar ✪✪ *Kantstr. 152, 10623 Berlin; tel. 313 80 52.* Classic French and international cuisine in intellectual/arty atmosphere. Popular meeting place for the young and seriously trendy. Open noon to 1AM daily.

Trio ✪✪✪ *Klausenerplatz 14, 14059 Berlin; tel. 321 77 82.* This elegant restaurant is adorned with modern art, and is very conveniently situated in a leafy square just opposite Schloß Charlottenburg. Open daily (except Wednesday and Thursday) 7-11PM.

Kreuzberg

Gropius ✪ *Stresemannstr. 110, 10117 Berlin; tel. 262 76 20.* A pleasant, airy café-restaurant in the Martin-Gropius-Bau specializing in vegetarian and wholefood dishes. Open 11AM to 8PM. Closed Monday.

Großbeerenkeller ✪ *Großbeerenstr. 90, 10963 Berlin; tel. 742 49 84.* Real German home cooking in an ancient cellar. Open Monday to Friday from 4PM until 2AM, and from 6PM on Saturday.

Hostaria del Monte Croce ✪✪ *Mittenwalder Str. 6, 10961 Berlin; tel. 694 39 68.* Copious portions of genuine Italian food in an authentic atmosphere, though there's only one set menu. Reserve in advance. Open evenings only, closed Sundays

Osteria No. 1 ✪ *Kreuzbergstr. 71, 10965 Berlin; tel. 786 91 62.* A lively ambience combined with delicious trattoria fare keep the regular young crowd flocking back for more. Reservations are highly recommended. Open daily noon to midnight, until 12.30AM Friday and Saturday.

Thürnagel ✪-✪✪ *Gneisenaustr. 57, 10961 Berlin; tel. 691 48 00.* Trendy if slightly pretentious vegetarian restaurant. The décor is neutral and soothing, although the prices tend a little towards the expensive. Nevertheless, reservations are advisable. Open daily from 6PM until 1AM.

Mitte

Beth Café ✪ *Tucholskystr. 10, 10117 Berlin; tel. 281 31 35.* A bistro atmosphere characterizes this small, friendly kosher restaurant situated in the heart of the Jewish quarter. Open 9AM to midnight Saturday to Thursday, closes Fridays at 3PM in winter, 6PM in summer.

Borchardt ✪✪✪ *Französische Str. 17, 10117 Berlin; tel. 203 97 150.* An elegant, airy restaurant with a twenties atmosphere, situated just off historic Gendarmenmarkt. The menu changes daily and portions are satisfying. Drinks are served until 2AM.

Café Orange ✪ *Oranienburger Str. 32, 10117 Berlin; tel. 282 00 28.* Always lively and extremely crowded, probably because of the excellent spaghetti sauces and the gorgeous pale orange and white stuccoed surroundings. It's a great place to stop for lunch, when the place is a little less busy. Open 10AM to 1AM daily.

Café Oren ✪ *Oranienburger Str. 28, 10117 Berlin; tel. 282 82 28.* A superb restaurant near the New Synagogue, offering meat-free Jewish and Arab specialities in elegant and soothing surroundings. The "Orient Express" is particularly recommended. Service is always efficient and friendly, and there's access for wheelchairs. Open daily from 10AM until 1AM.

Berlin

Ermelerhaus 1 ✪✪✪ *Märkisches Ufer 10, 10179 Berlin; tel. 278n 78 50.* Overlooking the Spree River, an elegant wine restaurant at the top of a winding baroque staircase offers a fixed-price menu which changes daily. Open daily from 11:30AM to 3PM and 6PM to midnight.

Französischer Hof ✪✪-✪✪✪ *Jägerstr. 56, 10117 Berlin; tel. 229 39 69/229 31 52.* A large selection of excellent French, German and international dishes is offered at this stylish restaurant just opposite the Französischer Dom. Choose either à la carte or from one of 10 daily fixed-price menus. The Hof is open daily from 11AM to midnight.

Opern Palais ✪-✪✪✪ *Unter den Linden 5, 10117 Berlin; tel. 200 22 69.* There are two restaurants and two cafés to choose from in the renovated palatial mansion just next to the Staatsoper: Operntreff, with Mediterranean-style cuisine and live music; Königin-Luise restaurant, offering elegant German cuisine; Operncafé with a selection of simple salads and a large choice of cakes; and Fridericus, specializing in fish dishes. Open from 8.30AM until midnight daily.

Reinhard's ✪✪ *Poststr. 28, 10178 Berlin; tel. 242 52 95.* In the renovated Nikolaiviertel, this lively bistro serves American-style food to a mainly business clientele. Open daily from 9AM until 1:30AM.

Restaurant Moskau ✪✪ *Karl-Marx-Allee 34, 10178 Berlin; tel. 279 16 70.* Formerly frequented by one-time GDR big-wigs, this restaurant now serves some genuine Ukrainian dishes to a more bourgeois set. Open daily from noon until midnight.

Turmstuben ✪✪ *Gendarmenmarkt 5 (in the Französischer Dom), 10117 Berlin; tel. 229 93 13.* The international menu includes excellent fish dishes, and there's an impressive selection of wines as well as a great view. The perfect place to dine after a concert at the Schauspielhaus. Open daily from noon until 1AM.

Further afield

Bamberger Reiter ✪✪✪ *Regensburgerstr. 7, 10777 Berlin; tel. 218 42 82.* A refined approach to Tyrolean cuisine, with some wonderful desserts. Friendly service. Reservations recommended. Dinner only. Closed Sunday, Monday, two weeks in January and three weeks in August.

Biberbau ✪✪✪ *Durlacherstr., 10715 Berlin; tel. 853 23 90.* Excellent German and French cuisine in a bourgeois atmosphere. Reservations are essential. Open to 1AM daily except Tuesday.

Blockhaus Nikolskoe ✪✪✪ *Nikolskoer Weg, Wannsee, 14109 Berlin; tel. 805 29 14.* German cuisine in a lovely setting overlooking the Havel and Peacock island. Open 10AM to 10PM.

Café Einstein ✪ *Kurfürstenstr. 58, 10785 Berlin; tel. 261 50 96.* This Viennese-style coffee house in Schöneberg buys in international newspapers which you can read in a delightfully literary ambience. Open Friday to Wednesday from 9AM to 10PM, 10AM to 8PM in winter.

Candela ✪ *Grunewaldstr. 81, 10823 Berlin; tel. 782 14 09.* Pizza and pasta are the staples of this unassuming Italian restaurant, which also offers a changing day menu. Food is authentic and the service good. Open daily from 5PM to 1:30AM.

Forsthaus Paulsborn ✪✪-✪✪✪ *Am Grunewaldsee, Zehlendorf, 14193 Berlin; tel. 813 80 10.* An attractive restaurant near the Jagdschloß Grunewald with a fine selection of game dishes as well as smoked Scottish salmon. Excellent view of the lake. Reservation advisable. Open in winter from 11AM until 6PM, in summer from 11AM to 11PM, Tuesday to Saturday; closed Monday.

Berlin

Hakuin I ✪✪✪ *Martin-Luther-Str. 1, 10777 Berlin; tel. 218 20 27.* Splendid curries and Buddhist vegetarian food in a tranquil setting, with the additional bonus of a no-smoking area. Open 6PM to 11:30PM weekdays (except Thursday) and Sundays noon to 11:30PM.

La Maskera ✪ *Gustav-Müller-Str. 1, 10829 Berlin; tel. 784 12 27.* A welcoming Italian vegetarian restaurant with interesting tofu dishes. Open to 1AM daily

Offenbach-Stuben ✪✪ *Stubbenkammerstr. 8, 10437 Berlin; tel. 442 24 94.* In Prenzlauer Berg. Theatrical décor, colourful, sometimes eccentric clientele. Reservation advised. Open to 2AM daily.

Restauration 1900 ✪✪ *Husemannstr. 1, 10435 Berlin; tel. 449 40 52.* International cuisine predominates in this select restaurant in the heart of Prenzlauer Berg. The wine list is good and the service attentive. Reservation essential. Open noon to midnight daily.

Rockendorf's Restaurant ✪✪✪ *Düsterhauptstr. 1, 13469 Berlin; tel. 402 30 99.* Berlin's top restaurant, in Waidmannslust with elegant Jugendstil décor. Reservation is essential. Closed three weeks in summer, two weeks at Christmas, Sunday and Monday. Open to 11PM.

Udagawa ✪✪ *Feuerbachstr. 24, Steglitz, 12163 Berlin; tel. 792 23 73.* Excellent Japanese cuisine. Reservation essential. Open 5:30PM to 11:30PM daily (except Tuesday).

Zitadelle ✪✪-✪✪✪ *Am Juliusturm, 13599 Berlin; tel. 334 21 06.* Medieval banquets are held every Friday, Saturday and Sunday evening. Reservation advisable. Open 6PM to midnight Tuesday to Friday, 11AM to 11PM weekends.